Nonfiction Books by Russell S. Smith

The Gun That Wasn't There

No Reason to Kill

One Policeman's
LIGHTS
and
SIREN

RUSSELL S. SMITH

This book is a work of nonfiction. Every effort was made to try to confirm each fact, but unless otherwise noted, the author and publisher make no explicit guarantees as to the accuracy of the information. In more than one instance, names and personal information were omitted for privacy reasons. The names of most persons-of-interest or those convicted have been changed for privacy reasons, and/or pseudonyms used instead.

The cover design is by Anne-Charlotte Patterson (Southern Combustion Creative, www.southerncombustion.com).

ISBN: 1449986137
ISBN-13: 9781449986131
Library of Congress Control Number: 2009914066

Acknowledgement

One Policeman's Lights and Siren is a collection of memories from my early police career. My thanks go out to all those who helped make this work possible, especially Dixie McAda, Vickie Reisner, Diane Wilson, and Joe and Louise Fields who assisted with record information; Caleb Denson, David Hermes and Deen Dickson for photography assistance; Areta Robinson, Kathy Robinson, Becky Smith, June Smith and Linda Smith who proofread the final drafts, and each police officer, retired or active, who helped verify the accuracy.

My special thanks to Joe Gibson, retired police chief and author of **Old Angelo**, for his comments on the back cover. A very special thank you goes to Linda Hermes for her thoughtful editing suggestions and to Anne-Charlotte Patterson who designed the cover.

In memory of those I worked with:

SAN ANGELO POLICE OFFICERS

Aubrey D. "Rusty" Smith ❋ George Riles ❋ John Pounds
Roy Gene McKnight ❋ Richard "Wayne" Heinze
Charles "Chuck" Richardson ❋ Gary Michael Kordek
Jerry Dean Watkins ❋ John David "Dave" Magee
Homer "Dean" Huddleston ❋ Gene Fly ❋ Sammie R. Goodwin
Forest Bailey ❋ James "Wesley" Smith ❋ Thomas "Tom" Allen
Lyna "Wayne" Phillips ❋ Terry Ripple ❋ Don Klinger
Clay Emert ❋ James D. "J.D." Wright ❋ B.C. Dominguez
Walter "Walt" Pierce ❋ Fred Roeder ❋ Pedro "Pete" Martinez
Johny Benavides ❋ Nestor Wuertenburg
James "Pappy" Jackson ❋ Timmy Franke ❋ John R. "Jack" Rees
William O. "W.O." Walker ❋ David "Jack" Beckham
Henry Landgraf ❋ James "Mac" McClellan ❋ Lee Roy Strickland
Roy "Jack" Jones ❋ Leon Webb

SAN ANGELO LAKE RANGERS

Ernest D. "Junior" Vaughn Jr. ❋ Johnny Jones

TOM GREEN COUNTY SHERIFF'S DEPARTMENT

Odell Wagner ❋ Ernest Haynes ❋ Loil "Bubba" Balentine
George Jaimes ❋ Raymond Meador ❋ Murry Dabney
Clint McNeely ❋ Richard Dyer

And to anyone I may have forgotten
with the passage of time.

Introduction

I GREW UP AT UVALDE where my world involved family, God, church, school, and our great outdoors. I loved to hunt, fish, play baseball and write. I graduated from Uvalde High School and attended Southwest Texas Junior College. I left college early to learn the mechanics trade at General Motors Training Center in Houston. While I worked for Don Friend's Wes Cooksey Motors, I met, dated and married Linda Alvey from Rocksprings. Three years later, in early 1976, not long after the birth of our son Ryan, we moved to San Angelo where I worked for the Schuch Motor Company (Pontiac-Toyota Dealership). My love of fishing led me to a career in law enforcement.

It was about midnight on a cool, clear summer night. The sounds of rushing water echoed through spillway walls that connected Twin Buttes to Lake Nasworthy. Lantern light allowed me to see the tips of two fishing rods that hung over the top, the handles locked under the luggage rack on top of our station wagon. The car was parked close enough so I could rest my feet on top of the concrete wall. Linda and Ryan slept inside as I lifted fish after fish from the depths about fifteen feet below. Then I heard the noise, the swooshhhhhh of a car accelerating.

The vehicle sped right toward us, moving down Spillway Road at a high rate of speed. I watched and wondered what the driver was doing. The car sped into a curve to my left and headed directly toward Lake Nasworthy. With only a large boulder and a few mesquite trees in its way, the speeding mass hit both and the car disappeared from sight.

I slid down into the driver's side window, started the car and drove toward the wreck. Linda awoke and I told her what had happened.

The front part of the 4-door sedan was submerged, the back held up by a broken mesquite tree. I dropped over the edge and down into the water below. I pushed the button and pulled, and the driver's door opened. The lone occupant was unconscious, his feet still below the steering wheel, and his head face down in the water on the passenger-side floorboard. He smelled like a brewery as I started to work his deadweight from the car and up the embankment to the road above. He came around and started coughing at some point and I told Linda, "Go get the police."

Slender with a ruddy complexion, the dark-headed man in his mid-forties stood several inches taller than I. His face had apparently hit the steering wheel (and possibly the windshield) because spots of blood dotted our clothes by the time Tom Green County deputies Mike McCarty and Wayne Armstrong arrived. "He kept wanting to go back down to the car, but I wouldn't let him because I was afraid he might drown," I told the officers.

They handcuffed the man and one of them blurted out, "He probably wanted to get rid of the gun." The guy was from out of town. He came here and caught his wife with another man, shot at them and was then chased by San Angelo police officers. Just before the deputies drove off, one said, "You know you ought to join our reserve deputy program."

Five foot four and two hundred fifteen pounds, I didn't think I was really in any shape to be a police officer. But the idea interested me, especially when I realized that newspaper ads no longer listed five foot seven minimum height requirements. My weight was still a problem, in my own mind, so I decided to get in shape.

We lived in the College Hills West Apartments. Each morning I jogged to Southwest Plaza and down Knickerbocker Road to the dealership. I showered in the make-ready stall and then dressed for work. Linda and Ryan picked me up each afternoon. Each night, after a small supper, I jogged around the block several times, then did wind sprints, took a shower and went to bed. This went on for months until I went to work for the automotive department of Sears Roebuck and Company.

Assistant store manager Jack Keller had recruited me with the promise of better benefits and 50% commission on all the work completed. This was a no-brainer decision because the automotive industry had just started to reduce the commission paid to their certified mechanics. Cecil Roe managed Sears' automotive department and Harry Curtis was the shop foreman.

I might not have entered law enforcement at all, except that Sidney Becknell was also a mechanic at Sears. His brother Danny was a San Angelo police officer and his father, Neal Becknell, was a reserve deputy with the Tom Green County Sheriff's Department. He and his dad both encouraged me to seek the reserve deputy appointment.

Linda and I had recently moved to a house on Clayton Street. It was about this time that I got up the courage to ask Tom Green County Sheriff Odell Wagner for his permission to join the reserves.

I was so nervous that day, wearing my Sears uniform and fearing the worst. Sears was located between the companion blocks of 100 West Beauregard and Twohig Streets; the Sheriff's Office was located behind the courthouse, a block away on Harris Street. I walked over there during a late lunch break.

Sheriff Wagner's smile was genuine and he made me feel comfortable. His demeanor reminded me of Uvalde County Sheriff Kenneth Kelley, a man I greatly respected, though Wagner wore a gun and Kelley didn't. He introduced me to Capt. Robert T. "Bob" Woolsey, the supervisor who ran the reserve program.

The Tom Green County Sheriff's Academy for reserve officers started months later. The reserve candidates all had fulltime jobs so the classes were held mostly at night. Sadly, Sheriff Wagner had a heart attack and died at the rodeo about two months before we graduated. Chief Deputy Ernest D. Haynes was appointed Sheriff.

Sheriff Haynes, Chief Deputy Loil W. Balentine, Captain Woolsey and Civil Captain Roberta Leidecker signed our graduation certificates on May 5, 1978.

Wagner, Haynes and Balentine were former San Angelo police officers. Woolsey was formerly with the Bexar County Sheriff's Department.

The Texas Commission on Law Enforcement Standards and Education issued my Reserve Officer (Peace Officer) License on May 1, 1978.[i]

* * *

1978 PHOTOGRAPH OF TOM GREEN COUNTY
RESERVE DEPUTY SHERIFF RUSSELL SMITH.
FAMILY PHOTO.

The Beginning

SHEETS OF HEAVY RAIN WERE falling so fast that I could hardly see. Even with bright headlights and the windshield wipers on high, my vision was greatly hindered as I drove onto a narrow bridge. Suddenly I swerved to miss a man in the roadway, right in front of my patrol car.

My Reserve Deputy memories include fear, fear of the unknown that was present while I drove to the Sheriff's Office for the first time. There was the scent of new leather (holster, belt and handcuff case); the sound of cartridges sliding into the cylinder of a .38 caliber revolver; gold "SO" lapel pins and a Tom Green County Sheriff's Deputy badge. There was also plenty of excitement, anticipation and that little bit of fear. What I didn't think about was the fact that I might accidentally, or purposely, ever take a human life.

The Tom Green County jail was upstairs, the main offices and dispatch downstairs. The building also housed offices for a constable and two Justices of the Peace (Judge Ruth Nicholson and Judge Richard Self). An ultra conservative county government didn't provide many resources. "We only had two deputies assigned to work nights, and four street deputies in the daytime," said Mike McCarty.

Memorable deputies that I remember were McCarty, Wayne Armstrong, George Jaimes, Tom Steckbeck and Norman Fisher. Curtis Smith served the civil papers. Murry Dabney, with Bert Bruton's help, ran the administrative end of the office. Night deputies were Ken Fleming and Jimmy Don Cox. U.E. "Pete" Skains and Bill McCloud were the criminal investigators. A good number of people worked in the jail. "I started in the jail and then went to the street," said McCarty, who was previously a pawnshop and finance company employee.

My two days off at Sears were Thursday and Sunday. I signed up to spend both at the Sheriff's Office. I drew Sunday nights and Thursday days. My first taste of the non-paying job was on a Sunday; Jimmy Cox was assigned to show me the ropes.

Cox's slow drawl, slight smile and dry wit complemented his offset cowboy hat, wire-rimmed glasses and western attire. The man stood half-a-foot taller than I, and the badge and gun seemed to be made for him. Once we were in his patrol car, he turned south toward Christoval. "My wife has cooked supper for us," said Cox.

Deputy Cox and I had two things in common. We were both 27 and we both had known Johnny Rodriguez before he was a country music star. I'd worked with the singer at a tire-test facility just after I got out of high school. Cox worked with him at Brackettville's Alamo Village, during the time that Rodriquez started his climb to the big time. That night I also learned that Cox had plenty of talent himself.

The painting in the deputy's living room nearly took my breath away. Though not a connoisseur of art, even I knew I was looking at something pretty special. The horse and landscape looked real and I didn't want to quit looking at it. "Boy that sure is a pretty picture," I said. Cox pushed the comment aside, said the painting was not good enough to sell. I've always wished I'd had enough gumption to ask him to sell it to me, and will forever wish I owned one of his paintings. (He painted the portraits of the former Tom Green County Sheriffs that are mounted on the walls of the Sheriff's Office today. They are amazing – the eyes seem to follow you around the room.)

Television and the movies portray an awful lot of lights and siren incidents in police work. Chases and high profile crimes seem to be the norm. My first night on patrol I realized that such events were not the rule, but rather the exception. Our time was spent with a stranded motorist, someone needing directions, and assisting a Texas Department of Public Safety Trooper with a drunk driver. We checked on a few convenience store clerks as the deputy introduced me to the southern part of Tom Green County. "We handle the calls outside San Angelo, the city police handle those inside," said Cox.

The night shift assignments were basically spent on preventive patrol and answering calls for service, but the day shift offered me greater insight into the workings of a sheriff's department. Deputy McCarty and I served warrants and either collected money owed or took the people to jail; George Jaimes and I took mentally ill folks to the Big Spring State Hospital; and inmates were escorted across the street to and from the courthouse. With so few deputies, day shift was a busy time, especially when a convict had to be taken to or brought back from prison.

Tom Green County had a lot of reserve deputies in 1978. "I think we had nearly forty reserves that year.[ii] Reserves handled the day shift calls on the weekends, and rode with the regular deputies at night," said Pete Skains. Of course, there were a few times when the regular deputies were not available and reserves handled the night shift by themselves.

Such a situation occurred one Sunday afternoon. Reserve deputy Pollye Smith, an elementary school teacher, and I were assigned to work the northern half of Tom Green County. It is one night I will never forget.

Neither one of us had ever worked by ourselves; we had always accompanied a regular deputy before. We left the Sheriff's Office about 6:00 p.m. I drove as we patrolled U.S. 277, parts of Quail Valley, FM 2105, U.S. 87 North and the streets in Grape Creek and Carlsbad. It was about midnight, as strong storms pelted the Concho Valley, when we left a convenience store at Grape Creek and headed west on FM 2288.

Luckily I was driving slowly. Otherwise, even with the bright lights and the windshield wipers, I might have never seen the man staggering across the two-lane bridge near Dry Creek Park. He was in the middle of the roadway and the car barely missed him. I activated the overhead lights and turned the patrol car around. I eased back past him and parked beyond the bridge, off to the side. Pollye Smith called it in to the dispatcher as I got out to investigate.

The man's slurred speech was cordial but revealed a strong odor of alcohol. He failed what field sobriety tests I could administer in the rain. Blood was visible on his right hand and on his clothes. He and his wife had had an argument; they were camped at Dry Creek Park. He'd cut himself slightly trying to get back into his trailer. His wife had the keys to their truck – inside the trailer.

The man was visibly drunk and a danger to himself; he was arrested for public intoxication and placed in the patrol car. After we drove into the park and checked on his wife, who said she was okay, we took the man to jail. This was my first arrest without a veteran officer with me. The date was May 22, 1978.[iii] More than thirty years later, I still remember the man's name and where he lived.

* * *

2009 PHOTO OF NORTH CONCHO RIVER BRIDGE ON FM 2288 NEAR DRY CREEK PARK. DURING A HEAVY RAINSTORM, RESERVE DEPUTY RUSSELL SMITH ALMOST HIT A DRUNK PEDESTRIAN ON THE BRIDGE IN 1978. PHOTOGRAPHED BY DEEN DICKSON.

Lights and Siren

Deputy Mike McCarty met me at the front door of the Sheriff's Office. "You're with me. Get your shotgun," he said as he headed toward his patrol car. Chief Deputy Bubba Balentine and a number of other officers followed us outside. It was about 5:30 p.m. on Sunday, August 6, 1978. I was about to experience my first drug bust.[iv]

My pulse quickened as soon as McCarty told me, "We're going to run a search warrant on an apartment on the west side of town." As we got close, my grip tightened on the Mossberg 12 gauge riot-gun that I'd placed barrel down across the seat beside me. My eyes moved into tunnel vision when someone announced over the radio, "One suspect just left driving east on Guadalupe Street," and they gave the description of a car that was just passing in front of us.

The dark-headed, bearded driver didn't seem to pay us any attention. He drove down about two blocks and stopped in front of a house. Just as he started to open his driver's door, we stopped just back and out to the side of his car. I was out, almost without thinking, and pumped a shell into the shotgun. "Freeze! Police!" I shouted.

Surprise was evident in the man's green eyes. Then his expression changed; I saw a look I'd never seen before, but would see many times during my law enforcement career. The 30-year-old man glanced down, to the right where a loaded revolver and a box of marijuana rested on the front seat. Then his shoulders dropped and he slowly raised his hands and stepped from the car.

McCarty handcuffed the dope dealer and placed him in our backseat. I took possession of the drugs and the gun (removing the shells) and placed them in our trunk. Another deputy arrived and started to help us inventory the car. Then we heard tires squealing, spinning on a different car, a green Mustang, leaving black marks and smoke behind as it headed south on Garfield Street. "Let's go," McCarty yelled. The chase was on.

The emergency lights and siren were activated as we weaved in and out of traffic, trying to catch and stop the hopped up Mustang. We went right, straight, then left, right, and finally ended up on Sherwood Way, the main drag, headed west from the intersection of Pecos and Sherwood Way.

I leaned out the right side window with my shotgun. Then I realized that people were parked alongside the popular roadway. We weaved around cars full of people. I dropped back into the passenger seat. The Ford turned south on A&M, then slid into the parking lot of the Westside National Motor Bank. The driver got out and raised his hands.

After the second suspect was secured, I asked the first, "What was that look you gave me when we first stopped you?" The man looked me right in the eyes and said,

"I was trying to decide whether I wanted to go back to prison or not."

* * *

"You know, we love doing this so much, maybe we ought to do it for a living," said Reserve Deputy Joe Gibson. The big man, former business editor of the San Angelo Standard-Times, owned The Minuteman Press, an offset printing company that offered a variety of services. We had become close friends while we were in the training academy. We were both hooked – law enforcement was in our blood.

I was working five days a week at Sears Roebuck and Company and spending the other two at the Sheriff's Office or out on patrol. Because of the schedule, my wife Linda, a stay-at-home mom, hardly ever saw me. So one day she said, "If you love doing this so much, why don't you do it for a living?"

Shortly thereafter, I asked Sheriff Ernest Haynes if he would sponsor me so I could attend the Concho Valley Basic Law Enforcement Academy. Administered by the Texas A&M University Engineering Extension Service, the school was held at the San Angelo Police Department training facility on FM 584, behind the airport.

Getting into the training was not the problem; the problem was that classes were held during the day, Monday through Friday, for six straight weeks. And I had a job. Automotive manager Cecil Roe arranged for me to work Thursday nights and Saturdays, "to keep your benefits," said Roe. Sears was across the street from the Star Lanes bowling alley. I worked there the other days, just trying to make enough money to make ends meet. But it wasn't enough – and I was plenty embarrassed when it was announced, the week before the school ended, that graduation would be held during a luncheon at Zentner's Daughter Restaurant on Knickerbocker Road. I was embarrassed because I didn't have the money to pay for the meal. Working at the bowling alley did not replace the former paychecks from Sears. I'd already sold one of my guns so I could feed my family and pay the bills. I sold another gun the Saturday before I graduated.

On Tuesday, October 3, 1978, I went to the Sheriff's Office about 7:00 a.m. I'd been catching a ride to the school with several deputies. Chief Deputy Bubba Balentine gave me some disappointing news. The Tom Green County Reserves were to be disbanded. He asked me for my badge and identification cards, and asked me to keep it between us until the others were told.

"Reserve deputy force dissolved," were the headlines of the San Angelo Standard the following Thursday. Staff writer Alan Sayre described how nine reserve officers had been released the week before, and quoting Sheriff Haynes, "due to the fact that a few in the reserve force did not agree with departmental procedures." Chief Balentine told the reporter that three new deputies would take up the slack when they completed the basic law enforcement class on Friday.[v]

The 240-hour basic law enforcement course was much more in-depth than the reserve training. It was taught by experienced people from the local criminal justice field, including San Angelo police officers Sgt. Fred Dietz (criminal investigation), Sgt. Kirby Poss (narcotics) and

Sgt. A.D. "Rusty" Smith (juvenile procedures). During the six-week course, I learned to have great respect for Academy Director Bud Raney, former Floyd County Sheriff, and SAPD training Lt. Tom Flowers.

Tom Flowers managed the police shooting range and training facility. He was a long tenured police officer who helped Raney put on the school. He was a big man who treated people the way one would want to be treated, and he worked hard to see that everything was as it should be. He also played a direct part in helping me enter the law enforcement profession.

One of the last things we did in the academy was to hold a "mock trial" at the San Angelo Municipal Court. Assistant City Attorney Mindy Boyce (Ward) was the prosecutor and attorney Melvin Gray represented the defendant. The imaginary case involved the arrest of a drunk in one of the local parks. I was one of the officers who made the arrest.

After I had given testimony and been cross-examined by Mr. Gray, I was allowed to leave the witness box. As I settled into a seat in the gallery, Tom Flowers tapped me on the shoulder and whispered, "Let's go outside."

I'd seen Lt. Flowers and another man, in a suit and tie, sitting at the back of the courtroom while I testified. In the foyer, Flowers introduced me to retired FBI agent Dick Burnett, San Angelo's Police Chief. After we visited for a few minutes, Burnett asked me to go to city hall, right then, to apply to become a San Angelo police officer. I did as I was told, but, at the encouragement of the personnel director, I also applied to be a San Angelo Lake Ranger.

Chicken fried steak, mashed potatoes and gravy, and tea; what more could we ask for as a graduation dinner! Oh yes, I forgot those wonderful onion rings. Fourteen officers graduated from the required peace officer academy on Friday, October 6, 1978.[vi] A newspaper article included my name with Tom Green County deputies Norman L. Fisher, Kenneth D. Fleming Jr., Louis A. Hargraves and Kelly W. King; San Angelo Police officers Edmund Cobb, George Lee, Claro Pena and Albert Turner; Mathis Field security guard A.J. Long; Concho County Constable Frankie McClure; Kimble County Constable Clarence "Robby" Robinson; Concho County Chief Deputy Brian Smith; and Johnny Ortega from Runnels County.[vii]

However, after we graduated I wasn't an officer anymore. I had daydreamed of working for Sheriff Haynes and getting paid, but it just wasn't in the cards. I went back to work in the Sears Automotive Center and, because I was still behind on my bills, worked at the bowling alley at night. Several weeks later, while I was working on a machine that manipulates the pins, they announced that I had a phone call.

"The city has hired Tom Steckbeck to oversee a Lake Ranger force[viii] that will basically work at Lake Nasworthy. They are going to keep the two officers that are out there (Ernest "Junior" Vaughn and Johnny Jones) and they have hired Wayne Armstrong. One position has not been filled yet," said Sheriff's Investigator Bill McCloud. "I'll throw your name into the mix if you are interested."

City Water Superintendent Tom Koederitz called a few days later. I accepted his offer to join his Lake

Rangers. He told me I would start on December 1, 1978.[ix] I dropped by the Sheriff's Office to tell everyone the good news. Before I left, Deputy Norman Fisher put his arm around my shoulders and said, "Always remember, that people are just that, people. Unless they treat you otherwise, treat them as you would want to be treated."

* * *

Reserve deputy force dissolved

By ALAN SAYRE
Staff Writer

Citing organizational and personnel problems within the Tom Green County Sheriff's Reserve, sheriff's department officials disbanded the backup law enforcement force Wednesday afternoon.

State regulations require that th[e] reserve officers work a minimum of [1] hours per month to maintain their leg[al] certification. As a result of this rule Ballentine said, the department occa[-] sionally was forced to allow two reserv[e] deputies to ride together on patrol duty.

County sheriff reserve force is disbanded

By ALAN SAYRE
Staff Writer

Citing organizational and personnel problems within the Tom Green County Sheriff's Reserve, sheriff's department officials disbanded the backup law enforcement force Wednesday afternoon.

Following a meeting with the reserve's board of directors, Sheriff Ernest Haynes said in a press release that "due to the fact that a few in the reserve force did not agree with departmental procedures established" the department had decided to disband the force t_____

STAFF WRITER ALAN SAYRE WROTE TWO STORIES FOR THE SAN ANGELO STANDARD-TIMES WHEN THE TOM GREEN COUNTY SHERIFF RESERVES WERE DISBANDED IN OCTOBER 1978. ONE APPEARED IN THE MORNING STANDARD EDITION (TOP) ON OCTOBER 5TH AND THE OTHER APPEARED IN THE AFTERNOON TIMES (BOTTOM).

RUSSELL SMITH BECAME A LAKE RANGER ON DECEMBER 1, 1978.
FAMILY PHOTO.

The Rookie

"IF THAT IS HOW YOU are going to react every time someone tries to push your buttons, then you probably need to give a lot of thought as to whether you really want to be a policeman or not." Wayne Armstrong.

"Rookie," according to Wikipedia, is a term used for a person who is in his first year of play of his sport and has little or no professional experience; anyone new to a profession, e.g. rookie cop. The term rookie has been modified as simply "rook," as a synonym for newbie.

People are not born police officers. Pinning on a badge and placing a gun in a holster doesn't make you one. Those new to the job put on those items and go out and perform as though they believe a police officer should. Then, after they gain experience, most get up one day and realize that they are police officers. It is really a moral and ethical state of mind that becomes very much a part of them. Until that happens though, they are susceptible to "Rookieitus," or the more ego-driven state that some call the "John Wayne Syndrome."

Lake Nasworthy was not inside the San Angelo city limits in 1978. The Lake Ranger force was implemented with the law that allowed governments to protect their water resources. Our jurisdiction included Twin Buttes, but our main emphasis was park and residential areas around Lake Nasworthy.

It was during one of those times when my partner, Wayne Armstrong, and I found a car parked in the roadway along Gun Club Road. Several cars were parked up and down the winding road; yet one was parked so that it was a hazard to traffic on the roadway. College-age men and women were in the yard of a nearby house.

I was riding shotgun so I got out to tell them that the car needed to be moved. Quickly the group moved toward our patrol car. The violator, the person who had parked his car in the street, took a leadership role by saying something like, "Shouldn't you guys be out fighting real crime?" Liquid courage helped fuel remarks from those with him and there was little doubt the guy was talking down to us.

I was immediately in the guy's face, well not really because he was nearly a foot taller than I. Instead of saying something like, "Oh yea, we better go do that, fight crime, but you do still need to move the car," and move on, I was eighteen all over again; giving the guy my two cents worth. Our strong discussion escalated and I soon dropped into the car and took a ticket book from the glove box. I wrote the guy a ticket for the parking violation.

Afterwards, Armstrong put the car in gear and we drove off. He didn't say a word, but he stopped at the stop sign at Knickerbocker Road. He put the car in park and turned toward me. His words were direct, "If that is how you are going to react every time someone tries to push your buttons, then you probably need to give a lot of thought as to whether you really want to be a policeman or not." Then he put the car in gear and we continued our patrol. He never mentioned it again.

I didn't get much sleep after I got home that night. I thought of Armstrong's words, those of the violator and about my own actions. I wrote WARNING across the ticket before I turned it in to Municipal Court the next day.

* * *

A few nights later, I was working alone when I saw a black Pontiac Trans Am, accelerating and decelerating, over and over again, as it left donut designs on the beach at Mary Lee Park. I activated my overhead lights and advised the Sheriff's Office dispatcher that I'd be out there.

The driver, a girl with long black hair, cut off the muscle car's engine as I shined a light into the car. She smiled, looked embarrassed, and the male front seat passenger said, "We're just teaching her how to drive."

I guessed the girl's age at sixteen, the speaking passenger at eighteen. I noticed a tall guy wearing glasses in the backseat. I told them to teach her how to drive right, not in the inappropriate way she had been driving, and, unbelievably, this rookie drove away.

Thirty minutes later, San Angelo police officer Bob Rike put out what was known in law enforcement lingo as a 10-65 message, "Be on the lookout for a stolen black Trans Am…" The car was later found in the water off a boat ramp several miles away. Needless to say, I had egg on my inexperienced face. The car's license plates and inspection sticker were both expired. The girl may have looked sixteen but she was just thirteen. Luckily I remembered what the back seat passenger looked like and picked him out of a junior high (yes junior high) annual. Sheriff's investigators Pete Skains and Bill McCloud identified each of the juvenile offenders.

* * *

My new job put us in dire financial straights. Our son was just two years old. Our daughter was six months old and we were making payments to Shannon Hospital and the doctor. I started selling my guns to help put food on the table and pay the bills. Deputy Mike McCarty, holding a deer rifle as collateral, loaned me a hundred dollars more than once. I had averaged over $350 a week take-home as an automobile mechanic. Two weeks pay as a Rookie officer translated into just under $350. When I took home that first paycheck, my wife said, "Is this for two weeks?" I confided, "Yes, this is for two weeks."

She looked at me and said, "If you are going to do this, I'm going to have to go to work."

Linda had a fulltime job by the time I was hired by the San Angelo Police Department several months later. This was just one of many sacrifices she would make as she stood by me and supported me during my law enforcement career.

* * *

RUSSELL SMITH'S ROOKIE POLICE OFFICER ID CARD PHOTO.

Memories from my early police career...

The names of offenders and certain details have been disguised to protect the guilty from paying another price for a crime they already paid for, or from embarrassing someone who doesn't need such an emotion today.

RUSSELL S. SMITH

* * *

The "10-16"

RAIN PELTED THE CITY STREETS as I joined Patrol Officer James "Pappy" Jackson my first day on the job. "121, 120, 10-16," the dispatcher began as she gave us an assignment that took us to a Greenwood Street address. Jackson regularly worked 121, the northwest area, and Billy Pool, our backup, regularly worked 120, the center Westside part of the city. The call sign "10-16" was a code used to signify domestic violence, one of the most dangerous calls in police work. "You just stand by, watch and learn," Jackson told me as I left the patrol cruiser. I heard people yelling at each other inside the house.

The experienced officers immediately separated the husband and wife. The officers listened, surveyed the situation and, after gathering the required name, date of birth, etc., watched as the husband gathered a few clothes and left the residence. Just before we stepped back into the rain, Jackson put his hand on my shoulder and said, "Always go with them to get their clothes. You never know when they might get a gun or knife instead." As we hurried to the shelter of the police car, Jackson said, "And watch their hands, the hands are what can kill you."

* * *

Months later, the dispatcher reported, "122, 124, 10-16, the mother reports her son beat her up." She gave us a Medina Street address that I knew was one of the small cabin-style houses located west of the Taylor Veterinary Hospital, not far off Bell Street.

"You come on in and take this kid to jail!" a woman yelled as I approached the screen door.

The wooden door was open, the living area dark. It took a few seconds for my eyes to adjust but I soon saw a small woman cowered down beside a chair in an opposing corner. "He beat me. Take him away!" she shrieked as she pointed toward a teenager, about my height and size, who was standing along the wall to my left. I smelled paint and saw tiny patches of silver above the kid's upper lip. I knew the kid was a "huffer," someone who sniffed paint or glue to get high.

"Let's go outside so I can talk to you," I commanded of the young offender. I stepped back and held the screen door open, leaving enough room for the kid to get by. As he moved between the doorframe and me, he grabbed the butt of my pistol and screamed something like, "I'm going to kill you."

The struggle for life and death did not last long. I soon had the fourteen-year-old face down in the dirt, out near my patrol car. Then I heard an animal-like scream just as I started to snap the second handcuff into place. I turned my head to see the mother running out the door, holding a lamp over her head. I grabbed my pistol, believing she was going to hit me, or kill me, but Timmy Franke drove up and she stopped. Her child had beaten her unmercifully, but the woman was still coming to rescue her baby.

Franke had dealt with the mother for years. "She's a heroin addict," he said as we put the son in the back seat of my patrol car. Later, at the jail, Franke noticed my badge was no longer pinned to my shirt. The kid had apparently ripped it off during the ordeal. Luckily, I found it mixed within the dirt and gravel back at a place I'll never forget.

* * *

The officers working day shift were offered many opportunities to work overtime on the night shift. Such was the case weeks later when the dispatcher sent two officers to an address on Millbrook Street. "10-16, man with a gun holding a woman hostage." Within minutes, nearly all the Westside units were at the location.

Patrol Sgt. Kirby Poss took control and assigned officers to set up a perimeter around the house about 10:00 that night. His order for me was, "You go down and cross over into the back, get somewhere so you can see the back of the house."

The house was in the middle of the block so, with shotgun in hand, I ran to a neighbor's house two doors down. I rang the doorbell and knocked hard, but I couldn't hear anyone inside. I quickly turned, ran to the next house and rang their doorbell. Dennis Friedrich answered the door. I told him what was going on and he showed me the way out past their dogs and into the back.

An electrical highline ran behind the suspect's house. Using one of the poles as cover, I started to report what I could see from my vantage point. Open curtains allowed me to see through sliding glass doors and into the living-dining area of the home. "I see the guy, drinking a beer, looking out toward the back fence. The woman is sitting at a table, talking to him but I don't see any gun."

It was just a few minutes later when Sgt. Poss asked, "All officers, check your holsters."

I reached for my revolver but my gun wasn't there. Apparently my holster strap was unsnapped; the gun had fallen out as I hurriedly turned and ran from the first house to the Friedrich's. An older resident, in her nightgown, had finally opened the door and found my Smith and Wesson pistol lying on her porch. Using two fingers, she had picked it up by the trigger guard and carried it to the nice policemen who were hunkered down behind their cars a few doors down.

Luckily, the domestic violence investigation ended with a positive resolution. But twenty-seven years later, Dennis Friedrich still remembered me losing my gun.

Memories die hard as Friedrich told a group and me one afternoon. It was during a book-signing event after my first book, **The Gun That Wasn't There**, was published. The book is the story of the Caveman Bandit who shot Terrell County Sheriff Bill Cooksey, and it describes how the Sheriff and Texas Ranger Alfred Allee Jr. bring the culprit to justice. "You're the only one who could have written it because you're the only one I know who has reached for a gun that wasn't there."

* * *

The Rules

I WAS GIVEN A THIN green rulebook when I was hired by the San Angelo Police Department in March 1979. I read through the pages and placed the binder in the briefcase where I kept the many different forms and equipment that I'd need to do the job. One of the rules read something like: An officer shall not accept anything but his salary for doing his job.

"122, 10-17 (meet with the complainant)," said the dispatcher who gave me an Era Street address. The wood-framed house was on the north side of the street, a few blocks east of Bell. A thin woman in her late fifties met me at the door. She pushed her gray streaked dark hair out of her face. "Would you watch after my house while I'm gone?" she asked.

The woman said she was sick; she had cancer and would be traveling to San Antonio for treatment. She would be gone for several weeks and was concerned that her daughter, a drug addict, would break in and take everything. "I don't have much, but I don't want to lose what I have," said the woman.

Later, after I'd assured the woman we would watch her residence, I wrote a "house watch memo" describing the circumstances of the woman's plight.

Sergeants read such memos, along with information about stolen cars, wanted persons and other crime related events, at a briefing just before the officers of each patrol shift went to work. The morning shift worked from 4:00 a.m. to noon, day shift from noon to 8:00 p.m. and the night shift from 8:00 p.m. to 4:00 a.m. I was assigned to the day shift when I talked to the lady about her concerns.

As a rookie, supervisors assigned me to work different areas of town when the more experienced officers had days off. But anytime I was assigned to the southeast area of San Angelo, except for my days off, I drove by the house, got out and checked the doors and windows, and then went on my way. Until one day when I turned the corner and there was an older car in the driveway.

"Everything is okay Officer, this is my mother's house," said the woman who came to the door when I knocked. Though she did bear a resemblance to her mom, glimpses of a former beauty were disguised by years of drug abuse. Most druggies are very adept at lying and she was a master. Tiny, constricted pupils told me she was a heroin addict.

Patrol officer Timothy Franke arrived and I opened the screen door and stepped inside. The boyfriend was in the mother's bedroom. The couple had apparently not been there long. The television was still plugged in, so was the toaster. The mother's dresser drawers were open but a search of the man did not reveal anything of value. The bathroom window had been pried open; the swivel lock was bent and broken. A tire tool was laid across the back of the commode. I did not arrest the daughter or her companion, but I told them in no uncertain terms they'd be taken to jail if they returned. After they drove away, we nailed the bathroom window shut and secured the house.

* * *

It was not too many days later, while I was working the northwest part of San Angelo, that I decided to check out the storage units on Glenna Drive, located just across from the soccer fields. Supervisors had told us during briefing that burglaries had been occurring in such places. As I turned in between the two buildings, I saw two men loading a television into the back of a blue hatchback car.

Upon seeing me, one of the men moved to the passenger side of the vehicle. The other man pulled down the overhead door and placed a lock on the hasp.

'What's going on," I asked as I stepped from my patrol unit.

"Just getting our TV," said the older man who held up a key.

As I walked between their car and the storage building, I heard a noise in the front passenger seat and immediately heard the older man tell the passenger something in Spanish. I understood enough that instinctively red flags went up in my head. My fingers unsnapped my holster strap and my hand went to the department issued Smith and Wesson model 67 .38 caliber revolver that was at my side.

The noise was a younger brother grabbing hold of the hatchet that he'd just placed beside the seat. It was the sound of him taking hold of it, then, after his brother's words, letting it go, that made me move to a place behind their car where I could watch them both. "Send a backup unit," I radioed the dispatcher.

"It is our storage unit," said the eldest sibling who provided me his driver's license. The DL showed a Corpus Christi address but the man said they had just moved here, that was why their things were in storage. He showed me that his key did open the lock.

With my hand still clutched on the pistol grip and the men where I could see them, I used my portable radio to call in what I knew was a driver's license number written in permanent marker across the back of the television set. The number did not match the one I had in my hand.

The backup officer was Wayne Phillips, a good-sized man who always had a stubby cigar in the corner of his mouth. Known as Mr. Phillips to those he regularly served in the northeast part of the city, he arrived about the time the dispatcher reported the driver's license number belonged to a San Angelo resident. The two men were arrested for burglary of a building. The oldest burglar, in his early 30s, was already on felony probation for burglary out of Nueces County.

There were a lot of nice things in the storage unit. They were there because the owner would soon move into a new house, but his former home had sold quickly, before his new residence was finished. The original lock, pried open, was up on the roof. Luckily, our victim knew to put his driver's license number on his most valued goods. It made it easy to locate him. Had he used his social security number though, that information would have not been readily available, if at all.

After we booked the two men into jail, I thought about the younger man and the hatchet. I thought about what he might have planned to do with it. Years later, when I watched the Brian DePalma film The Untouchables, I thought about this time in my life, and others, when Sean Connery (playing a Chicago Policeman) said to Elliot Ness (played by Kevin Costner), "Well then, you just fulfilled the first rule of law enforcement; make sure when your shift is over that you go home alive."

* * *

Several weeks later I was sent back to the house on Era Street. It had been six weeks since the daughter had broken into the house. "I know your working another district, but the woman asked for you by name," said the dispatcher.

The mother looked tired. She had lost weight. A scarf hid that part of her head that would normally fit under a beautician's hairdryer. A bright flower-covered apron was tied across the front of her dress. A warm smile grew across her face as she opened the outside screen door. "Thank you so much for not arresting my daughter," she began, "because you know I would have bonded her out, would have had to spend money I really didn't have."

As I sat there for a few minutes, the woman told me about her experience with the disease. She told me about her life, about a little girl who fell victim to the scourge of illegal drugs and about her neighbors and the neighborhood that was her world. One of the neighbors had actually told her what happened after her daughter broke into the house. Finally, she stood and headed toward the kitchen, moving through an aroma that had caught my attention when I first entered the home.

"I cooked this for you this morning," she said as she returned holding a still warm German chocolate cake. "To thank you for what you did."

She didn't know it, but my grandmother used to make German chocolate cakes for me when I was a kid. With the coconut and pecan filled chocolate covered frosting, it was my favorite. Yet, in the back of my mind, I was thinking about the rulebook that read, "An officer shall not accept anything but his salary for doing his job." But there was a look in the woman's eyes, and a tone in her voice that said it was very important to her that I accept her gift.

I parked right in front of the police department, rather than in the back where officers normally parked. Sgt. Wesley Smith gave me a critical look as I moved past the front desk and headed toward the Chief's office. I sat the cake on the receptionist's desk. "I need to see the Chief," I said as I moved to a nearby chair, clutching the green rulebook in my hands. I understood the chain of command, but I figured he'd be the one to suspend me for accepting the gift.

Chief Burnett appeared in the doorway wearing a gray suit and dark tie. He listened as I told the story about first meeting the woman, dealing with her daughter and finally my reluctance to not accept the gift. His facial expression did not betray his thoughts, though once he did push his dark rimmed glasses back up on his nose. After I finished, his eyes winced and his body language told me, "Here it comes."

Our stocky gray-headed leader walked toward me, grabbed me roughly at the collarbone and, as I looked up at him, said in his gruffest tone, "I'll tell you what I am going to do…" But then his sour look gave way to a slight grin, and he finished with, "I'm going to eat the first piece."

(Retired FBI agent Richard J. "Dick" Burnett had unseated Wesley Smith in attaining the San Angelo Police Chief position in 1978. The Ohio native and former WWII pilot had spent the previous 13 years in the FBI's San Angelo field office. I didn't know it then, but he'd only been Chief for just over a year. Dick Burnett resigned in November 1979. He ran for and was elected to the Texas House of Representatives (1981 - 1989).

* * *

"The Crazy Nudist!"

"KILL ME, MAN! KILL ME!" The young woman screamed as she shook her head from side to side. I told her that we were not going to hurt her. But she had other ideas, or did she?

"Gloria's tearing up her mother's house again," the dispatcher reported in a tone that left little doubt that we'd been to the residence before. Gloria is not the woman's real name but she was someone generally considered as mentally unstable. Previous calls involved her walking along the highway exposing her privates, or about her fighting with her mother. This day, she was fighting with her mother again.

The mother met us in the front yard. Her green smock-style dress was ripped, her left eye swelling and blood dripped from her lips. She brushed her hair away from her face. "She ran out the back," the woman said as she panted and tried to catch her breath. "I've never seen her this bad, she tore up the whole house."

Gloria had done just that; the living room looked like a cyclone had hit it. Pictures were broken and on the floor, three legs were broken off the coffee table and the couch was turned upside down. Two holes were in the wall next to the door leading into the kitchen. The small kitchen table joined the trail of violence that led to the back door.

A blood trail led us out through the back yard, across a barbed wire fence and into the field behind the house. The young woman was hiding in a clump of brush. The look in her eyes left little doubt that she was in an unstable state of mind. Blood seeped from the knuckles of her left hand.

Officer Billy Ward and I knelt some distance away. We tried to talk to her, but she displayed the passion of a lion backing away from its trainer. She kept wiping blood on her blue tee shirt and, at times, kicked her feet like a five-year-old child having a tantrum. Several times she unsnapped and snapped a piece of her clothing. Each time we'd say, "Now Gloria, keep your clothes on." She'd counter with, "You're just like my mother."

It took about five minutes to calm her, but just like flipping a switch we finally helped Gloria to her feet and escorted her back to the house. She was calm, her expression totally different and she had agreed to go with us to see a doctor. It was working out to be one of the easiest solutions we'd ever had with her. Until her mother burst out the front door.

"You stupid girl," the mother screamed. "You've ruined my house, my things. Don't you ever come back!"

Gloria instantly reached for my gun, but I drew my body away. She screamed, "Kill me, man! Kill me!" I told her we weren't going to hurt her. Her eyes had "that look" again as she grabbed a stainless steel cooking pot, full of dirt and a dried up tomato plant, off the front porch.

"I'll make you kill me," she screamed as she started to swing the pot in my direction. I ducked but the pot caught Sgt. Fred Roeder on a hand he'd raised in defense of the weapon.

We immediately took the woman to the ground and handcuffed her. Even though she was restrained, the woman kicked out at us for several minutes. She finally calmed down and we helped her to her feet. I held the cuffs with two fingers and guided her to the curb. I'd parked across a busy street and we had to wait several minutes before all the traffic passed. Finally the traffic cleared and we walked across the street to my patrol car. I opened the back door and she eased herself into the backseat.

"10-95 to county with one female," I told the dispatcher as I pulled away from the curb. (10-95 is a police code for transporting prisoner.) I logged the mileage, which was something we did each time a female was transferred from one place to another in a police car.

Gloria was quiet for several blocks until she sat up and put her lips against the metal screen that separated us. As I glanced back at her, she looked directly into the rear view mirror and whispered, "You know Officer, if I was really crazy, I'd have stepped off that curb in front of those cars and taken you with me."

* * *

Night Shift

I WAS IN A HOMICIDE investigation training class sitting behind Lt. James T. "Teddy" Long and Sgt. Kirby Poss. I told the supervisors I enjoyed working overtime on nights. It was very busy and things really happened after the sun went down. I asked how I could get transferred permanently to their shift. They had me write a transfer request. Patrol Captain Forest L. Bailey transferred me the following weekend.

Night shift was as different as night from day. Officers regularly went from one call to the next. It was very busy. Experience came quickly at night, even the knowledge that some officers didn't belong there. I soon learned several things: Bad things happen in threes, criminal and abnormal behavior may escalate with a full moon, and things do crawl out from underneath rocks after the sun goes down.

* * *

The Little Guys

ROOKIES ARE USUALLY EAGER TO jump into a situation, to bring calm to chaos, or right a wrong. Policy would dictate that an officer wait for backup, and not doing so is a "rookie mistake." San Angelo had its share of tall, imposing men on the police force, and it was always good to find the likes of Dan Gray, Jake Young or Detective Dave Caudle assisting with a call. Each man stood the same height and knew how to bring closure to things that were otherwise out of hand. Such was the case when I was called out on a domestic disturbance.

The walls of the trailer house did little to hide the sounds of the man and woman who were inside cursing at each other. Normally an officer would have waited for a backup, but I was a rookie. I could only hear unhappy folks who might be in the process of hurting or killing each other. I used my metal flashlight to let them know I was there.

Tears streamed from the eyes of the heavy-set woman who opened the door. "You take that SOB to jail, that's where he belongs!" screamed the wife who was terribly, visibly unhappy. She raised a fist toward a tall husky man standing in the kitchen, and the couple's tirade started all over again.

She was yelling at him and he was yelling at her. Anger was in their eyes as the middle- aged pair started to move toward each other. I quickly moved between them and pushed them away from each other. She was pushing one way and he was pushing the other. They were yelling at each other, and I was yelling at them trying to calm them down, but they were so mad that they didn't want to listen.

These events usually had something to do with money, alcohol, drugs, infidelity, or specific matters important to one of the parties, but all these years later I don't remember exactly what started their argument. What I do remember is that these two people were so upset that they were not paying any attention to me. I had just become a minor obstacle as they yelled at each other, made threats and tried to hit each other.

I was at a point where I was trying to decide which one of them to take down, to arrest and get it over with. I knew that as soon as I did, the other would be all over me, resisting and saying how dare I arrest their spouse. I had my arms outstretched pushing them back and they were swinging, until the trailer house groaned and leaned to one side.

All movement stopped. Quiet came to the inside of that living room-kitchen area. All of our eyes were trained on the trailer house door. It opened and the body of police officer Dan Gray, all six foot five and about doorway wide, filled the open space. In his deep bass voice he commanded, "Any problem here?"

"Uh, no sir," said the husband, "I was just going to get a few clothes and leave."

* * *

The Coach

THE GREEN IMPALA WAS PARKED down a side street in a low water area that hadn't seen rain in many months. I'd never seen a car parked there. I pointed in its direction just as the brake lights offered evidence that the vehicle was occupied.

Rowe Wallace was my partner. It was a night when I was showing him around the part of town that formed my patrol area. He was a fine young man who had a slow, quiet manner about him. He was the kind of person my dad always told me not to pick on when I was a kid. His interests were his wife, their son and police rodeos. We discussed these things, the weather and crime related matters.

I cut my lights and turned in behind the car. I turned on my overhead emergency lights and my bright headlights. A man's head was visible against the driver's headrest. My partner and I both looked at each other after we saw a young boy raise his head out of the man's lap.

Wallace radioed our location to the police dispatcher as I stepped from our patrol car. When I got to the driver's side window, I leaned down, looked at the boy, and said "Young man, you get out of the car and go back to the other policeman." I asked the driver for his driver's license. I have never forgotten the man's demeanor. He was calm, collected and had it together. He explained he was the young boy's coach, and that the kid's parents were getting a divorce. He said the kid was upset and he was just consoling him, that the kid was taking it real hard. I asked the man to step from the car. I talked with him for several minutes. His body language didn't give a hint to his lying, nor did his eyes. He sounded totally believable. I asked him to stay by his car.

My partner and the twelve-year-old boy were at the back of the patrol car. The youngster was leaning against the trunk. I positioned myself where I could watch the coach but was somewhat facing the kid. I looked into the kid's eyes. I gave him one of those looks, the kind of look that makes kids quit doing what they are doing, the kind of look that lets a person know all your attention is on them. "Now just what the hell is going on?" I asked in a low but firm tone, as though I was talking to my own five-year old child at home, as though I had caught him doing something wrong.

The boy's eyes filled with tears and, at first, I didn't think I understood him right. "What did you say?" I asked as though I didn't hear him the first time.

"Before he takes us home," the boy sobbed, "he makes us give him a goodnight kiss." The boy was crying and his chin was on his chest. I told the kid everything was going to be okay and left him with my partner.

The coach was as cool as ice. He'd apparently had his story made up long before I'd asked for his driver's license. "Is there something wrong?" he asked in one of those tones that you normally hear from folks driving 55 through a school zone.

I told the coach that we had a juvenile detective coming to the scene, that it was common procedure when we found a juvenile out so late without his parents. He calmly offered, "Well, they know he's with me. I'm his coach."

Night Detective David Caudle and Juvenile Detective Bruce Kiser arrived within a few minutes. Both were seasoned investigators. Caudle was a big man with a direct manner. Kiser had built quite a reputation, years before, as a narcotics detective. Neither man told us what we wanted to hear. "Let the coach go," Caudle said as he explained they needed to get a statement from the child first. "We can always get a warrant later," said Kiser. I cut the coach loose, and we drove the kid to the police department.

Thirty minutes later, we crashed a slumber party that was chaperoned by the coach. Our kid had been the only one who couldn't spend the night, and his parents were not getting a divorce. He told us most of the team was at the party, spending the night with the coach.

We interviewed the kids and wrote their names, addresses and phone numbers down in our police notebooks. We told the boys we were just checking to see if they were okay. As we left the residence, the coach followed us outside. I kept thinking about my little boy, about how normal this coach looked and acted, about how I was feeling inside, and how I felt about not being able to make an arrest.

It was about this time when the guy spoke, "You act as though I've done something wrong." He spoke as if he were making a statement, rather than a question. His tone left little doubt that he thought he was above all our attention.

I'd just gotten a new rechargeable, metal flashlight for Christmas. Never before had I ever wanted to violate anyone's rights. I turned toward the coach and looked up at him, right into his eyes. I didn't speak because I knew better, knew I'd lose it. I gripped the flashlight in its holder. I sensed my partner's presence beside me.

We had both just listened to how a guy seduces little boys and I'd never felt this way before. Luckily, as if it was fate, Patrol Sergeant Larry Unger drove up and the coach went back inside.

I told Sarge what had just happened. "It's kind of hard to keep from letting cases like this get to you," said Unger. He went on to tell us that that was why we were here, to find and build cases against guys like this, to protect the innocent from guys like him. He also told us, "What goes around, comes around and he'll get his."

We drove back to the police department and phoned all the parents of the children. Each one said the same thing. "Oh, our kid's all right, he's at a party with his coach."

The following week, all kinds of good people (preachers, bankers, other coaches, teachers and people from the coach's church) called or made their way to the police department to voice their support of the coach. They said we had the wrong guy, that the coach was just a great guy. It was apparent that those good folks had not witnessed what Officer Wallace and I had witnessed.

After an intensive investigation by Detective Kiser, it was not long before the coach was indicted on six counts of sexual abuse of a child. He pled guilty to one count in a plea bargain that placed him on probation. It was an agreement that neither my partner nor I agreed with, but the detective said the parents didn't want their kids on the witness stand; they just wanted it over.

The detective told us the coach was not supposed to be involved with kids as long as he was on probation. He also told us that what goes around, comes around. He was right.

Nine years later, District Attorney Investigator Diane Wilson developed evidence that the coach was at it again. The coach not only violated his probation on the first charge, he ended up indicted on the new charge. He was finally sentenced to prison.

* * *

Angel Dust

ILLEGAL DRUGS WERE NOT PART of my childhood. I was
naïve about such things until Police Sgt. Kirby Poss
taught us about illegal drugs when I attended the basic
law enforcement academy. He really kept our attention
as he showed us the actual substances and allowed us to
smell burning marijuana. He educated us about the ills
and wherefores of commonly abused prescription medi-
cines, marijuana, methamphetamine, heroin, cocaine
and phencyclidine, a drug known as Angel Dust that he
said, "Can give the user superhuman strength."

The detective's instruction led me to research phencyclidine. Always a writer, I began writing a paper for
the notebook I had to turn in by the end of the school.
I felt my findings were suitable for a police magazine
and sent a copy to Police Product News, one of the top
law enforcement magazines in the country. I was really
disappointed when they sent me a rejection letter in
the mail. "I can't believe they wouldn't use it," I told my
friend Joe Gibson.

Gibson and I had gotten to know each other while we
were reserve deputies. I knew he was a former business
editor of the San Angelo Standard-Times and author of

a nonfiction book entitled **Old Angelo**. He also owned
The Minuteman Press. After reviewing my work, he said,
"You don't have anything to put in your resume, so give
the story away if you have to, to house organs, something
like our reserve newspaper."

The story appeared in the August 1979 issue of
Reserve Law News. My first article ever was entitled
PCP, and ended with a poem.

ESP about PCP

My first trip on Angel Dust,
Turned out to be my last,
I really wasn't in a rush
But now my life has passed.

"Now just throw a different beginning into it, and
include that you have been published in your cover
letter," suggested Gibson. I took his advice, placed
a hook at the beginning of the story and put it in
the mail.

I don't really know if words could describe the feeling
that came over me when I opened my mailbox in January
1980. The white envelope was about half an inch thick.
Inside were two copies of The Law Officer's Magazine,
Police Product News, February 1980 issue. Tears came
to my eyes when I saw the cover; a blonde-headed woman
was dressed as an angel, holding a shovel beside a head-
stone that read PCP OVERDOSE. In red letters at the
bottom were the words, "Angel Dust, A Hell Of A Way
To Go."

Angel Dust, in large letters, and my name highlighted an article that began on page sixteen:

Two killed and many wounded: A sniper opened fire on spectators at the 84th Battle of Flowers Parade in San Antonio, Texas on April 27, 1979. After a gun battle with police, the sniper was killed. The autopsy revealed the sniper had been under the influence of Angel Dust. Angel Dust? What is Angel Dust?

Angel Dust is another name for Phencyclidine, PCP for short. It is also known as Rocket Fuel, Super Joint, Peace Weed, Hog, Peace Pills, Dust, Dust Joint, Crystal, KJ, Parsley, Flakes, Goon, Killer Weed, Animal Tranquilizer, Super Weed, Elephant Crank, Soma, DOA, Ad Nauseum and Sernylan.

PCP began as a legal drug during the 1950s. It was used as an anesthetic for surgical operations performed on humans and as a tranquilizer and anesthetic for animals. Medical authorities soon realized that there were too many dangerous side effects on humans and it was removed from the market in 1965. Phencyclidine, under the trade name Sernylan, is still used as a veterinary tranquilizer and anesthetic for animals.

The two basic ingredients of Phencyclidine are Piperdine and Cyclohexanone. Since both drugs are widely used in industry, they are readily available.

Only one percent of the Phencyclidine found in drug abuse is obtained through veterinary sources. The majority of it is produced in laboratories, both professional and home type. Availability of ingredients, the minor tools needed to produce the drug and the high profit realized, all contribute to make PCP a growing problem.

Phencyclidine acts on the central nervous system and may either stimulate or depress, depending upon the individual and the amount taken. PCP is listed as a depressant under the Controlled Substance Act.

PCP can be eaten, injected, snorted, or smoked. You can become intoxicated on PCP just by being near someone smoking it. Some users sprinkle it on parsley or other leafy foods and eat it; some inject it like a heroin addict; some snort it like a person who uses cocaine. Others sprinkle it on or combine it with marijuana and either smoke it or inhale it, with the last method being the more common choice.

Effects can be felt within one to five minutes. Small doses may give a "high" for four to six hours while a two to four-day period is needed before a person returns to normal. Large doses just multiply the time involved. If a user starts using a certain amount and continues the same, soon he will have to use a greater amount in order to get the same effect.

PCP is rapidly taken from the blood and leaves the body through the urine. There is one exception: Traces left in the fatty tissue can become active at any time. A user could be somewhere months later and suddenly experience a "flashback."

High blood pressure, jerky movements of the eyeballs, loss of muscle coordination, slurred speech, blank stares, numbness and bloodshot eyes are some of the symptoms a person experiences under the influence of PCP.

Distortions in perception and the sense of movement mean that the user may not be able to distinguish up from down; while the inability to verbalize, difficulty in concentration and a feeling of estrangement mean that a user may feel as if everyone is against him or as if everyone feels superior to him. Since PCP was originally developed as an anesthetic, the user may not feel any pain.

Convulsions, psychosis, violent change in personality, and even death are effects PCP may bring upon the user. Some have found that effects lasted five years or more after they stopped using the drug.

The drug does not act the same on different users. The following are just a few examples:

A twenty-five year old college student gouged his eyes out with his own hands because he thought that he had seen something terrible. Later he could not remember what he had seen.

A thirty-seven year old actor, who was arrested in connection with the hillside strangler case, told reporters "I was smoking Angel Dust and I'm not in control of my speech."

One individual killed his father, mother and grandfather.

A fifteen year old, troubled by hallucinations, hanged himself in his garage.

A twenty-six year old killed his mother. Afterwards he had no memory of the incident.

Users have been burnt and/or injured but were unaware of the problem until the effects of the drug had worn off.

Some users have killed after smoking just a few joints.

Chronic users, in a violent condition, sometimes believe they are superman and have superhuman strength.

Users have jumped off cliffs or buildings.

Users have drowned, some in as little as two inches of water.

Some users have been hit by cars while they were walking down the middle of the roadway.

While believing they were God, the devil or one of their messengers, users have killed, then mutilated their victims.

Users have become blind.

Users have died.

The list goes on....

PCP can be found in many crude forms. It might be in the form of a tar-looking substance, in pill form, in liquid form, or in a dust form, PCP can be found in any color. As a rule, it would take a chemist to distinguish exactly what the substance is. PCP might be found in a mixture of several other drugs, such as marijuana, hashish, hash oil, LSD, mescaline, etc. Some dealers sell PCP to users as if it were THC, LSD, or mescaline.

After looking at the beautiful cover, reading the words of my story and dealing with the elation of the moment, I finally noticed a white envelope from Dyna Industries, Inc. inside the mailbox. My first paycheck was for fifty dollars.

* * *

"120, 128, unwanted subject at Showdown."

It was a weekend night. Showdown had had a rock band and the group was in the process of tearing down their equipment when I arrived. "We've got to be in Houston tomorrow night, so we've got to get a move on," said the band's leader who pointed toward a man leaning against an overhead doorframe, next to the vehicle they used to carry their equipment. "The guy says he's going with us, he's adamant and kind of scary."

Loud music from a jukebox had replaced the band, along with the common noises inside such a place: cue balls breaking the rack, people jeering, waitresses yelling "last call" over the normal chatter and the clinking of beer bottles and glasses. A large crowd and cigarette smoke helped me decide to approach the guy from outside on the parking lot.

The dark-headed guy was lean and about six inches taller than I. Though it was cold outside, he wore jeans, lace-up boots and a polo style pullover shirt. I guessed his age in the early twenties. "What's going on," I asked as I approached and stood about three feet away.

"Just waiting," the man said in a firm tone as he turned to look at me. He had a set look in his eyes. It was a stare that made me think he was looking through me, not at me. His eyes were bugged out a little, but otherwise his mannerisms didn't concern me.

"I need to see some ID," I said, and the man's left arm immediately struck out and hit my left chest. The strike felt more like a running back's stiff arm, rather than a swing and follow through. Needless to say, he and I were soon intermingled in a battle to take control of one another. We fell out in the parking lot and I ended up behind the guy, holding him around the neck, my legs around his waist. He was amazingly strong and kept repeatedly pulling my arms away, arms I'd replace when he tried to remove my legs. I did good just to hold on. He was yelling like a madman, words and phrases that didn't make any sense. He seemed to be lashing out at others who were not there. I was never so glad to see the backup officer when he arrived, even more glad to see the handcuffs on wrists behind the suspect's back. It was quite a chore getting them there.

The man did not get any better in jail. He did not sleep for days and cursed and threatened the Judge when he was arraigned. He yelled repeatedly about things no one could understand. Word finally surfaced that the young man was recently discharged from military service because he was under the influence of phencyclidine. He was apparently dusted, under the influence of Angel Dust, when we fought. With his great strength and bizarre behavior, I was lucky the man had not reached for my gun.

* * *

RUSSELL SMITH'S FIRST LAW ENFORCEMENT ARTICLES WERE
PUBLISHED IN RESERVE LAW NEWS (1979) AND POLICE PRODUCT
NEWS (1980). THE TOPIC OF EACH ARTICLE WAS PHENCYCLIDINE,
A DRUG THAT WAS COMMONLY KNOWN BY THE STREET NAME
OF ANGEL DUST. 2009 PHOTO BY CALEB DENSON.

Culwell

"122, ASSIST 123 WITH A DWI, Culwell by the tracks." The clubs (bars that sold alcohol) had just closed. The other patrol unit had been out there for a few minutes already; I'd heard him report his traffic stop over the radio and I was nearly there. The flashing lights of the police car were visible as soon as I turned off Bell Street. A blue Mustang was parked in front, on the south side of the street but facing west. I noticed a man in the backseat of the patrol unit, the driver already in custody. The police officer was talking to a pretty passenger in her mid-twenties.

The woman's long brown hair fell down her back to her waist. Wearing high heels, she stood almost five foot ten inches. Her blue, long sleeve shirt was open at the top, none of the buttons fastened, the bottom tied together beneath ample breasts. Her arms were crossed underneath, trying to keep warm in the coolness of the night air. An exposed midriff and long legs were set off by a pair of red shorts; a piece of clothing known as hot pants in those days. She was smiling, talking to the policeman, trying to talk him out of what he had in mind.

"He's pretty drunk," the officer said to me as he looked toward the man in his backseat. "She's had a little too much to drink too. Take her to jail for PI (public intoxication)."

The woman then turned her attention toward me. Her eyes, even in the poorly lit area, could have melted any suitor's heart. Her smile turned into a pout, and she purred, "You aren't really going to arrest me, are you Officer?"

"Do you have any guns, drugs or bombs hidden anywhere on you," I asked her, just like I asked so many people during my career.

"No, I don't," she whimpered as she held her hands out toward me. Normally we handcuffed everyone behind their back, but I thought - where in the world could this woman have a weapon hidden with so few clothes. I snapped the metal bracelets across her wrists and guided her into the backseat.

An observer might have thought we were the best of friends while I drove toward the jail. With her fingers clasped into the cage, the sectioned metal wire that secured the backseat from the front, she laughed and flirted and talked all the way to the breezeway at the back of the police station.

The radio crackled just as I opened the door to let her out. "122, have her searched. Drugs were found in the car."

The woman was even more striking in the well lit area of the jail. I removed the handcuffs and both jailers stepped up to the booking desk, eager to fill out the forms necessary for their guest. "Name and date of birth?" one of them asked.

We didn't have a female officer or jailer on the night shift, so a dispatcher was called upstairs to perform the strip search. A mature redheaded woman, who knew what the score was, took our drunk into a tiny kitchen and shut the door. It was just a few minutes later, and only after a few forceful words were heard beyond the barrier, that the dispatcher and the woman re-appeared.

The dispatcher didn't find any illegal drugs, but she did hand me an extremely sharp straight razor. In a tone that made me realize she was not happy about the whole ordeal, the dispatcher said, "It was open, hidden in a sheath she has attached right above where she ties the knot."

Turning to the woman, I said, more as a statement than a question, "I thought you told me you didn't have any weapons on you."

The woman's eyes were no longer warm. They narrowed, her smile disappeared and she retorted in a quiet but forceful tone, "And if you wouldn't have been nice to me, I'd have cut your (expletive) throat."

* * *

Morning After

Tomorrow, I'd drive home
If today, I could remember
Where yesterday, I left my keys.

Russell S. Smith
Copyright 1984

The Loud Noise Call

POLICEMEN REGULARLY GET SENT TO loud noise calls late at night. They normally find people playing their music too loud, people partying outside or situations of domestic violence. I don't remember very many of those calls, but I do remember a few.

"122, 130, loud music…" I knew the location was a rent house near Goodfellow Air Force Base; it was something you learned when you worked the same area for a while. It was after midnight when Officer Luke Allen (130) and I pulled up in front of the residence.

Luke had worked the south-side rover district for a good while. He was a policeman by night and a photographer by day. He taught me how to develop my own film and to produce prints – the old way in today's standards. He let me use his darkroom when he didn't need it.

The music was excessively loud. Even from the curb, we could hardly hear ourselves talking without raising our voices. The bass was bouncing off the sides of opposing houses, the rock music definitely loud enough to wake up the neighbors, and keep them awake.

The wood-framed structure was a corner house that faced south. Several steps led up to the porch. I knocked on the doorframe, but no one answered. I stepped off the porch, to the left, and could easily see through thin white curtains that stood behind a large picture window. I motioned for Luke Allen to come look at the unoccupied living room.

Like most houses, there was a couch, chairs and end tables, lamps and a large stereo, but there were also marijuana plants hung over the inside doorways and on string attached along the walls. Marijuana buds were visible within a large bowl sitting on the coffee table. Joints, hand-rolled cigarettes, lay beside a nearly full ashtray of those already consumed.

As we stood there, a door opened just inside a hallway. A partially clothed man danced into the living room. Wearing just shorts, with his arms aimed toward the ceiling, he was spinning, dancing, singing to the beat of the music. I used my flashlight to knock again.

Luke held the screen door back as I met the man who opened the inside barrier. A marijuana smell flowed into the clean outside air. Realizing, after a second or two, that we were policemen, the man tried to slam the door in my face. He was too slow to act, and he was taken into custody.

Bright growing lights and large marijuana plants were found inside an adjacent bedroom closet. Foil covered windows kept the neighbors from seeing the illegal activity.

Narcotics detectives used a pickup to remove the marijuana pot-plants and a mass of evidence they recovered from the house. As we walked outside later, the neighbors across the street, on each side, started to clap.

This was not the first time and it wasn't the last time that drugs were found during a loud noise call, but it was surely one of the most memorable.

* * *

The Trailer

"135, 10-17 (SEE THE COMPLAINANT)," said the dispatcher as she gave me the lot number in the Stardust Trailer Park. The 135-patrol district included everything north of downtown between the river and North Chadbourne Street. The trailer community was located just north of 23rd street, between North Bryant and what is now Martin Luther King Blvd. The tall, thin jittery man standing outside, who kept looking back toward the trailer door as I approached him, immediately blurted out, "They killed someone in there. Cut them up. I think they are still in there."

The man could not stand still, kept moving around, looking toward the trailer door. He was definitely concerned about what or who was inside. The man spoke very fast, "I came home. Found blood all over the tub. A piece of somebody is still in there. Whoever did it is still in there. Don't want to go in there, until you get them out."

The man's brown shoulder length hair was uncombed, unkempt. His eyes were dilated so far out that I could not tell the color of his eyes. I noticed rings on each of his constantly moving fingers; rings designed as little knives that could cut a person to pieces. The man kept moving, shaking and scratching himself all over.

I radioed for another unit, and when he arrived, I told the man, "For our safety, I need to search you for weapons, and then I'll get the people out of your house." There was a folding-blade knife in each pocket of the man's coveralls; two in the back, one along each thigh and one in each of the upper front pockets, six in all.

The living room was just inside the front door, the kitchen to the right. Beer cans and cigarette butts were everywhere. Trash, orange juice containers, papers and odds and ends were visible on the coffee table, kitchen table and on the floor. Knives were found on the kitchen counter, on the floor by a living room chair and along the upper framing material by the entrance.

"They are back there," the man said as he motioned toward the back hallway with his head. With guns drawn, we slowly made our way to the first bedroom. It was a mess. The bed wasn't made, the sheets in disarray, and trash, beer cans and cigarette butts were throughout. There was no one in the room, under the bed or in the closet.

The bathroom was down the hall to the left. The door was nearly closed. I pushed it open with the barrel of my gun and peered around the corner.

"See the blood, see the blood all over the tub!" the owner shouted out. He and the other officer were behind me down the hall but his words sent chills up my spine.

The vanity and toilet were to the left. The bathtub was to the right, the faucet setup along the wall that was away from me. A wide stain started at the top of the tub and continued down to the drain. I could see other stains, as I moved into the room, but none of them were blood. The colors were yellow, orange, brown and gray, the same colors one sees with hard water, shampoo and soap left too long on the ledge.

"See! They left a part of the body in the tub!"

The man was right about one thing; there were tiny pieces of something in the bottom of the tub. If I were to guess, they were tiny pieces of a hot dog.

When I returned to the hall, the man blurted out, "They must be in my bedroom."

The master bedroom was much more orderly than the rest of the house. More knives were on top of a dresser, but otherwise no one was visible in the room. Slowly I opened the closet door and shined my flashlight inside. "No one here," I announced.

"They must be under my bed; check under the bed," said the man from the doorway.

No one was under the bed. Yet in plain sight were several plastic bags of an off-white powder that I guessed were methamphetamine, an illegal drug that stimulates the central nervous system. Known as crank, crystal and speed back in those days, users commonly sniffed, smoked or injected the substance. The presence of syringes indicated the latter. By that time in my career, I had already learned that addiction could lead to weight loss, paranoia and, in some cases, psychosis. I knew that our complainant had all the signs of severe psychosis that could lead to delusions and hallucinations.

A narcotics detective tested the powder and it was methamphetamine. The man was arrested and taken to jail for felony possession of an illegal controlled substance. During the booking process, the psychotic man actually thanked me for helping get the people out of his trailer.

* * *

K-C Sales Company

A CLEAR SKY, BIG MOON and subfreezing temperatures set the stage for the night. It was so cold that most people just stayed home or stayed inside the clubs until they closed. It was dry; moisture would have only made it worse. The police radio was pretty quiet until just after 3:00 a.m. when the dispatcher reported, "124, 122, alarm at K-C Sales on South Chadbourne."

The propane business was located in the 3400 block of South Chadbourne, on the north side of the roadway between the river and Christoval Road. The K-C Sales office-shop building set back and was met on two sides by a fenced yard that secured metal propane tanks and equipment used in that type of business. A large 3000-gallon capacity truck that was in the middle of the yard. Security lights lit up the otherwise quiet area.

Patrol officers regularly approached such alarms as quietly as they could, in hopes they could catch the burglars in the act. Officer Don Gallion (124) and I both shut off the headlights of our patrol vehicles before we arrived on scene. He drove toward the gate just west of the building. I went down the other side, to the east so we had the yard in a crossfire, as one might say, and could see the back of the building. Nothing was moving, and nothing looked visibly out of place.

The front of the building was secure, the gates were locked and we didn't have the keys. We knew fences and locked gates didn't stop burglars, so we climbed the fence and made our way into the work area.

We couldn't see anyone behind the building, but someone could have been hidden around the vast supply of propane tanks inside their yard. We spent a few minutes looking around, before Don walked back to the structure and used his flashlight to check the windows at the back of the shop area. "Someone broke the window," he yelled, "but there's not enough room to get inside."

The propane truck was the closest thing to the building, so I shined my flashlight underneath. Two men were wedged up around the long drive shaft. Our burglars had just started to break in when they heard us coming.

I don't know who was the most glad to see the owner when he finally arrived to unlock the gate. Was it Don and I or the handcuffed burglars? I don't really know but we were all glad to feel the heat inside our patrol vehicles that we'd left running.

It was just past four in the morning by the time I left the area and headed north with one of the burglars. He was fairly amenable, especially when a red Trans Am came out of a side street and started weaving from side to side as it headed north on Oakes Street. "Are you going to stop that drunk?" the man asked.

I activated my overhead lights and hit the siren. The sports car continued for several blocks, then finally bounced into the curb and stopped near Fort Concho.

I radioed in the license plate number and location to the dispatcher, and flipped my headlights on high just before I got out.

As I started toward the Pontiac, I noticed the driver lean over to the right, across the center console, with his head turned back toward the driver's window. I placed my hand on my revolver and forcefully ordered the driver out of the car. He was crying and very drunk when he stepped out. I didn't find any weapons when I patted him down and assumed I'd just over-reacted after finding the two men hidden under the truck earlier. As I placed the cuffs on him, the man in his late twenties slurred, "I'm sorry. I just got probation for DWI yesterday."

Patrol officer Debbie Ward pulled up just as I placed the drunk in the backseat with the burglar. "Would you mind inventorying the car?" I asked. Policy dictated that the property inside an arrestee's car be listed, along with documenting any damage, on a multiple-sheet inventory form before a car was towed for safekeeping. She knew I would normally have already gotten off, and she had just started her shift. She gracefully agreed and I headed toward the jail. I had only driven about two blocks when Officer Ward called me on the radio. "I found a Clerk™ .32 caliber revolver in the right front floorboard."

* * *

Untitled

Someone stole your belongings.
You said you'd file charges,
If we found out who did it.
You said that whoever did it
Belonged behind bars,
But you haven't said a word
Since we arrested your son.

Russell S. Smith
©1984

The Backup

"120, 121, 128, 10-10 (FIGHT) inside Scratch's Corner," announced the dispatcher.

Scratch's Corner, 1425 W. Beauregard, served a clientele of various social status. Muscle cars, pickup trucks, Volkswagen bugs, Harley-Davidson motorcycles and other assorted vehicles were normally parked outside. I was a block away when the call went out.

The parking places were full so I turned on my overhead lights and parked at the edge of the street, near the corner, blocking a few cars in the process. Entering the northwest door, I thought a "whack" sound was someone sending a cue ball into a rack on one of the pool tables in the eastside of the business. Cigarette smoke hung in the air and rushed at my lungs as I realized the "whack" sound was louder than the Charlie Daniels Band singing <u>The Devil Went Down To Georgia</u> on the jukebox. Longneck beer bottles set along most of the tables. A group of people cheered someone on inside their good-sized circle.

I pushed my way through, listening to the cursing and "whacking" that was happening right in front of me. A man wearing cowboy boots was kicking a near-unconscious body on the floor. The man was kicking at the victim's head; blood was everywhere.

I grabbed the offender from behind, slipping an arm around his neck and pulling one arm up behind him. Taller than I, he lost his balance with the arch in his back. I screamed, "Police," into his ear and his resistance waned, but the circle tightened as I tried to move toward the outside door. Those who had been egging the man on surely didn't want their friend to go to jail.

I kept a tight hold and pushed, wishing that I'd waited for my backup before going inside. Then I felt space behind me, and those around me started to move away. I made it to the front door, released the man's arm and yanked the door back. A flashlight hit my index finger while it was still against the doorframe. An officer had the metal flashlight in his hand as he was starting to enter the business. I would lose the fingernail days later, but I was really glad to see the officers who arrived.

With the suspect handcuffed and in the backseat of my patrol car, we started to get the names of any witnesses who might have seen the aggravated assault take place. Just like we heard so many times over the years, in crimes from simple assault to murder, nearly everyone interviewed said they were in the bathroom when it happened; others said they were playing pool and/or just not paying attention.

An employee had called in the fight. Agents with the Texas Alcoholic Beverage Commission frowned on businesses that didn't report such crimes. The bartender and several waitresses were interviewed. One waitress, who would have normally never given the police the time of day, a woman who we'll call June for the sake of this story, said, "Russell, David over there had your back. He was swinging a pocket knife back and forth; he kept the others off of you."

"Were David and the victim friends? I asked her.

"No, I don't think David knew the guy who was hurt," answered the waitress.

Patrol officers do not always know the outcome of their arrests. Unless they are called to testify at trial, or they read the disposition in the newspaper, they may not know the end result. The only thing I do remember is that a fireman working the ambulance told me it didn't look good, that the man might lose one of his eyes. Don't know if he did or not, just that he took a terrible beating.

Several months later... "121, 128, 10-56 (drunk) inside Showdown, see the manager."

The club owner was waiting outside when we arrived, and he said, "The guy just came in and passed out."

The drunk was sitting at the end of the bar. His arms were up on the counter, his head down between them. The music was loud but you could still hear the guy snoring. He was sleeping. He was searched for weapons and a folding-blade knife was removed from his back pant's pocket. Then we took hold of the fellow and started to turn him toward us.

He was really drunk. A strong odor of alcohol spewed forward as he tried to speak in what amounted to very slurred speech. You could hardly understand him and what he said didn't make any sense. But he had a big smile on his face. He was a happy drunk who I recognized as David "Backup."

Normally the man would have been arrested and taken to jail for public intoxication. He was definitely not able to take care of himself and could have gotten splattered had he wandered into the roadway. But this was David "Backup," the man who had helped me months before.

I had to help him out of the club. He couldn't stand without swaying or falling, so I put his arm around my neck, similar to the injured helped off the field at football games, and guided him to my car. I had parked just outside the door with the passenger side toward the club. I didn't handcuff him and placed him in the front seat. I latched the seatbelt across his body and shut the door. He was snoring again before I drove off.

I had decided to give David a break. He had helped me and I appreciated what he had done. I knew where he lived and was giving him a ride home. We were on Avenue N near Angelo State University when I heard him come around.

Through his roadmap eyes he was trying to visualize the things around him. His head turned as he stared out the right window, through the windshield and then his eyes settled on the microphone of my police radio. Quickly, surprisingly so, he grabbed the microphone and brought it to his lips. "I know hooooow-www to do thissssssss," he slurred, as he somewhat yelled, "Brrrrrraker one nine, cuuuummmm back good buddddddy."

I quickly hit the off button on the radio and let him serenade me to his house. Luckily, someone was there to help me get him inside.

Outside, after I turned the radio back on and told the dispatcher I was back in service, officers started to click their mikes all over the city. In the police psyche, clicking the microphone was a way we gigged each other without saying anything. I was gigged plenty that night but, after what David had done to help me, it was well worth a little ribbing.

* * *

The License Plate Thief

PATROL LT. TEDDY LONG ASSIGNED me as a West side rover not long after I was transferred to the night shift in 1979. Working in one area allowed me to get to know people who worked in restaurants, bars and convenience stores. Soon I knew many of their work schedules, when the businesses closed or when the employees got off. On this particular night in the summer of 1980, Tish Wilson's white pickup was not parked where it should have been for that time of night.

The Colonial Convenience Store was in a small strip mall (3 stores) on Southwest Boulevard just south of the overpass at Loop 306. The development of the Southland Subdivisions was underway but was far from completed. I normally checked the store just before it closed. This was normally the blonde manager's final night to work; she'd be off the next few days, and then back to work again. Her little pickup was always parked out front, just north of the store's large glass windows, but it was not there.

The store was set back off the street and was elevated so my eyes were actually leveled with the bottom of the front glass doors. In the dark, just south of the store,

I noticed a car that I'd never seen there. I turned my headlights on bright and turned into the parking lot.

The elevation and the angle of the parking lot allowed me to see the rear license plate and the space between the car and the ground. I immediately noticed movement on the ground at the front of the car. "I'll be out with a kid stealing license plates," I told the dispatcher after giving her my location.

San Angelo had been having a rash of license plate thefts that were apparently used to replace those on stolen cars, cars mostly taken for joyrides though some were traded for drugs. I left my car's engine on, my shotgun on the floorboard and started to walk toward the front of the other car. Suddenly a man, much taller than I, jumped up and ran around to the back of the store. I vaguely remember yelling, "Stop, police!" as I started to pursue him on foot.

I ran by the car, quickly glanced down where the suspect had been moving around and then made the turn behind the store. The convenience store was on the south end and two other businesses attached to the north. An arroyo and tall grass were to my left and the tall lanky fellow was running ahead toward more tall grass and the Loop beyond.

I was nearly to him when he entered the grass and I heard someone yell in a very commanding tone, "Police, freeze! Lay down or I'll..." The mind is a very complicated thing. I didn't know how complicated, or wonderful, or talented, or scary until that night. My mind had gone into slow motion after I saw the mask lying in front of the other car. I don't remember drawing my pistol or placing it over the top of my flashlight, just like I'd been taught and repeated so many times during training. I don't remember yelling those words but I was the only policeman there. Though it was fairly dark, everything was visible, including the man as he turned, himself as though in slow motion, with his right hand drawing a pistol out in front of him.

The man's eyes were on me as he twisted, his hand and the gun headed around toward me, and then his fingers opened and the pistol flew from his grasp. I saw every little detail, as though I was watching it on television, watching it in slow motion. I watched him lie down amidst the yellow grass that reached higher than my head.

He did as he was told, moved his feet out, hands out as I started the felony takedown that I'd been taught and re-enacted so many times. His head was turned such that he could not see me, I had him where I wanted and needed him to be to make the arrest. Then as the slow motion of my mind moved back to real time, I noticed the hammer on my double action revolver slowly move back into the set position. (Squeezing the trigger of a double action revolver causes the hammer to move back until it releases and falls, allowing the firing pin to hit the primer that ignites the cartridge, sending the bullet out the barrel.)

I shuddered as I realized I'd been just a smidgen from shooting the guy. Had the guy's hand kept coming, I realized I would have at least double-tapped him (shot twice) like I had been taught in school. From six feet away and with his tall frame, I knew where the bullets would have gone. I handcuffed the guy, but left him lying there. I stepped back, removed the portable radio from its holster on my belt as said, "10-31 (crime in progress), one in custody."

Sgt. Mike Morris was working Channel One in the dispatch office, probably while a dispatcher went to the bathroom or took a break. I will never forget his voice saying, "10-9, Unit calling, you're breaking up. Go to your car."

I don't remember who the officer was, but an officer who was close enough to hear the radio transmission, reported immediately, forcefully, "Armed robbery, one in custody!" Then, I heard one and then two, and more sirens start to wail from across the city. It was a good feeling to know that help was on the way in such a situation. I was worried because of what I hadn't seen as I drove up; I had not seen any clerk inside the store. I wondered, "Was she alright? Was this guy the lookout and could someone else still be inside?"

I picked the guy's pistol up off the ground. I helped him to his feet, and kept him between the store and me as I walked him back to my police car. I was just placing him in the backseat when the first backup arrived.

"I didn't see a clerk," I told the Officer.

We made our way into the store's front door, as quietly as we could, careful not to activate the bells that hung from a string attached to the arm at the top. Keeping our heads down, we checked behind the counter and down the isles but found no one. We made our way to the storage room but no one was there either. Slowly, I opened the door that led into the cooler.

The brunette clerk was kneeling on the floor. She was pulling beverages from boxes and placing them on the shelves, getting the store stocked for the next day.

She smiled, and swiped a lock of hair away from her eyes, as she said, "Oh, I didn't hear you come in." She had not been robbed and was unaware of anything that happened outside. She was filing in for the manager who had taken ill.

Detective Clay Emert came to the scene that night. He sat against the hood of my car and listened to my play by play of what had occurred. He removed the shells from the robber's .38 caliber revolver, a firearm that contained the same Winchester ammunition that I was carrying in my gun. He finally told me, "Book the guy for attempted capital murder and for attempted armed robbery."

Back at the police station, Emert read the guy his rights and talked to him about the ordeal. "He was just starting to walk in and rob the place when he saw your police car come under the overpass. He said he wasn't going to shoot you. He gave me a written statement so I dropped the attempted murder charge," the detective told me later. Ultimately, the suspect pled and was convicted of attempted armed robbery.

I called my Dad at Uvalde after I got home that morning. We talked about all kinds of things, but I didn't mention the robbery arrest until he said, "I know you didn't call and wake me up just to talk about the weather, so what gives?"

I dreamed about that night, many times over, for several years. I didn't stop dreaming about it until I became a narcotics detective in 1983.

* * *

THE COLONIAL FOOD STORE AT 4321 SOUTHWEST
BOULEVARD. SAPD CRIME SCENE PHOTOGRAPH.

MASK FOUND LYING IN FRONT OF THE CAR (ABOVE) AND
THE REVOLVER AND GLOVES THE ROBBER HAD WITH HIM
(BELOW). SAPD CRIME SCENE PHOTOGRAPHS.

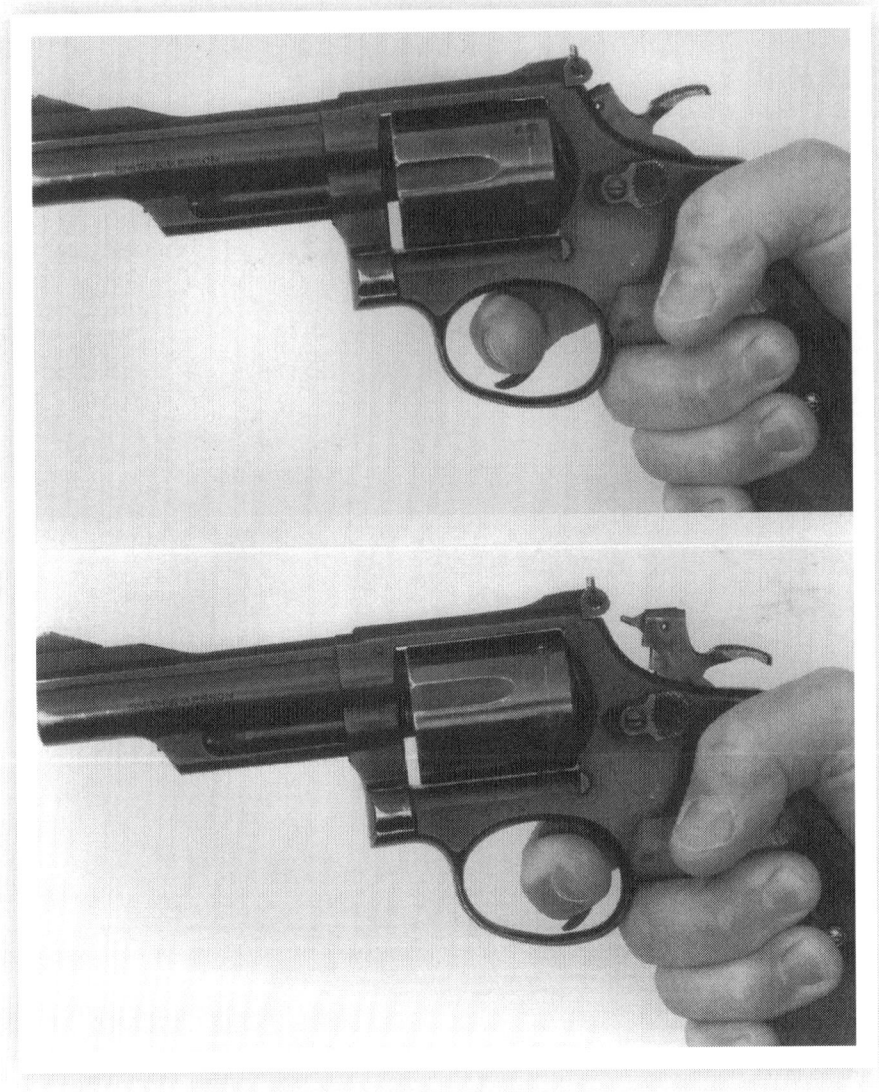

SQUEEZING THE TRIGGER OF A DOUBLE ACTION REVOLVER
CAUSES THE HAMMER TO MOVE BACK UNTIL IT RELEASES AND
FALLS BACK, ALLOWING THE FIRING PIN TO HIT THE PRIMER
THAT IGNITES THE CARTRIDGE, SENDING THE BULLET OUT THE
BARREL. 2009 PHOTOGRAPH BY RUSSELL S. SMITH.

Untitled

Sometimes,
The handwriting on the wall
Is never fully understood
Until it is translated
Into granite.

Russell S. Smith
©1984

The Shooting

"121, 128, 120, SHOOTING IN the parking lot at Showdown, one down." Showdown was a nightclub on the north side of Sherwood Way, just west of Arden Road. You could hear excitement in the dispatcher's voice as she followed with, "Ambulance already on its way."

I looked at my watch and realized the club was just closing. I was working the east side of town, but, as with any in-progress violent felony crime, I started heading toward the location, just in case. It was not long before the officers started to arrive there, then I heard, "He's on foot, running east across Arden Road." He gave the suspect's name. He was someone most of us were familiar with; someone we'd dealt with in the past. The officer sounded like he was running, partially out of breath. I hit the accelerator.

The radio continued to crackle with reports of, "He's behind that building; he's behind that house," as the pursuers tried to catch and arrest the shooter. The hunters and their quarry were moving east somewhat parallel to Sherwood Way.

I parked behind a portable building located on the northeast corner of the practice field at Lee Junior

High School. Another patrol car was already there. As I walked around the north end of the building, I could hear the sounds of the chase to the west. Dogs were barking, things banging and people yelling. I started to move toward it, when I heard a deep voice say, "Let him come to us!"

Officer James Hendry was leaning against the wooden building, holding a shotgun, the barrel in his left hand; the butt against his thigh. He was hardly noticeable, hidden by a dark shadow below the glare of nearby streetlights.

A tall man, Hendry always reminded me of Lucas McCain on the Rifleman television show. The former Wyoming and Coleman (Texas) police officer was a quiet man with a reputation as the best "building checker" in town. He regularly found open doors on commercial buildings in the southwest part of the city. Most of the doors were just left open by an owner or employee, but once in a while burglars were brought to justice. When Commodore computers were developed, he also began to take the job home with him.

The experienced officer cared about his work and the community. On his own time he started to produce computer sheets that showed where the burglaries and major crimes were occurring. Using information from the handwritten crime reports, he developed his own way of identifying trends to prevent crime and/or catch the criminals. But on that night, he was waiting for a criminal to come to him.

The sounds of the chase moved closer and closer, and finally an image appeared across the expanse of the large open space between Campus Street and where we stood. The thin man was running, all out, but you could tell he was exhausted. He'd come out of the area near San Antonio Street, cut across diagonally and was heading toward the intersection of Guadalupe and Childress streets. He was running right toward us.

Within seconds, the man had covered the distance. "Now you can go get him," Hendry said just before he racked a 12-gauge shell into his pump-action shotgun and yelled, "FREEZE, POLICE!"

The sound of metal sliding against metal has a way of getting a person's attention. The man stopped in his tracks and slowly raised his hands. He complied with every command: keep those hands up, kneel down on the ground, lie down on the ground and spread those legs. Hendry kept the shotgun on him until I had him handcuffed. He was searched but didn't have a weapon on him.

I worked the other side of town so I never knew much about what happened with the person who was shot. I only knew that Officer Hendry and I caught the guy the other officers were chasing. Common procedure was that, within a few days, a Judge would read the suspect his rights and set his bond. (A bond is required to ensure that a person will appear in court to answer the charge against him.) A car accident claimed the man's life not long after.

* * *

The Mistake

POLICE CHIEF TRAVIS JOHNSON TRANSFERRED me into Crime Prevention in 1981. My duties included administering the Crime Stoppers program. The anonymous tip-line was answered in our office during regular work periods, but after hours and on weekends police dispatchers answered the phone. "Russell, I know it's late, but some guy says he wants to talk to you; he says he has something really good that he'll only tell you," said the dispatcher. It was a phone call that would lead me to make one of the biggest mistakes in my life.

The caller wanted me to meet him in the grocery store parking lot across the street from the police station. Once I got there, he told me he wanted to show me where large quantities of marijuana were being brought into Tom Green County. I could smell alcohol on his breath but he didn't appear intoxicated. He wanted us to use his truck so that no one would see him in a police car, unmarked or not. Reluctantly, I agreed.

The man drove out a major highway and pointed toward a paved driveway. I took notes, drew a map and was interested in what might be the final result. "A helicopter brings in the drugs, right across the treetops," said the man, as he followed with, "Now I'll show you the other place."

Within minutes, we were headed out Arden road. We were out past the FM 2288 intersection before I realized the man's demeanor had changed. He was sweating and his voice started to break, occasionally, as he said, "You know there are some people who are really not happy with you. They are not happy with Crime Stoppers and the arrest of one of their friends."

I knew Narcotics Detectives had arrested the man he was talking about with pounds of marijuana. I knew he and his friends had been very violent in the past. I didn't know exactly where the man was planning to take me, but I realized his goal was not to show me where large amounts of narcotics were hidden. I had my portable radio in my left hand and slid my other hand onto the butt of the revolver pressing against the small of my back. Needless to say, I encouraged the chauffer to take me back to the traffic signal at FM 2288 and Arden Road. He had tears in his eyes and said he was sorry as I got out.

After he drove away, I pushed the talk button on my radio and said, "Headquarters, I need a ride."

"10-9, Unit calling, you are breaking up," said the dispatcher who couldn't understand what I was trying to say from that location.

I walked to the convenience store at Arden and Glenna and finally got a ride to the police station. I don't know if I ever told anyone about this incident, until now. It was a rookie mistake, and a lesson that I never forgot.

* * *

Untitled

And though
I have been scared
And known fear,
Like most people
Just dream about;
I will persevere
For I am guided.
Thank you Lord.

Russell S. Smith
© 1984

If The Police Only Knew

WOMEN WERE STANDING, TALKING IN small groups when I entered the room. My contact waved and said, "We've saved you a place up front." The dinner tables, set for about forty, were arranged in a rectangular fashion. I was to speak about our Crime Stoppers program for twenty minutes and leave ten for questions. As the women started to sit, I heard a young, well-groomed woman say, "I may leave as soon as we eat because I don't have anything to do with crime." But she was still there when I stood to begin.

"If the police only knew. Have you ever known or heard about someone who has done something illegal, and ever said those words?" My opening stopped the little side-by-side chatter that normally filled such social gatherings. "If you have, and you don't want to tell a policeman, then Crime Stoppers could be the answer, because people who call Crime Stoppers can remain anonymous."

"Crime Stoppers was the brainchild of an Albuquerque police detective named Greg MacAleese. He used the media to re-enact and advertise an unsolved murder, a murder that was solved almost immediately thereafter because of an anonymous phone call. Afterwards, Crime Stoppers programs developed all across the nation. Each involves a partnership between law enforcement, citizens and the media. Rewards are offered for information that leads to an indictment in felony crimes. Callers may remain anonymous if they call the San Angelo program at 658-HELP, which is 658-4357."

I spoke to many such groups after I became the Crime Prevention officer and coordinator of our local Crime Stoppers program. On this particular day, I spread the aforementioned history and a few local success stories over twenty minutes. Then a question came from the back of the room, "But do you just kick in a door and arrest people, just because you get an anonymous phone call?"

"Solving crime is much like putting together a jig-saw puzzle. The caller may or may not have the piece of information needed to make an arrest. Officers have to investigate each call first," I told the group, and then continued with, "Let me give you two examples."

I explained that during one Crime of the Week, we had asked people to call us about suspicious activity in their neighborhoods. We told them to be on the lookout for things like a lot of people coming and going from a residence on a regular or irregular basis. "A few cars might not mean anything, but ten or more a day, that stay just for a minute or a few, could mean drug dealing or something else that is illegal, or maybe not."

The first example was about a call we received about cars going to and from a house in the Santa Rita area. "People come to the house every Thursday afternoon, there must be twenty or more and they don't stay long. Each person leaves with a bag," said the caller.

"Can you get license numbers for us, of the cars that come and go?" the caller was asked. "No, the house is too far away, and I've done all I'm going to do."

The large house was located on the West side of the street. As I drove by the following Thursday afternoon, I noted the license number of a car parked way up in the driveway, beside the residence, as though it might belong to the owner. I drove onto a side street, turned around and parked so I could see the house, but hopefully so those who came and went would not see me.

About four, a car drove into the driveway and a young woman got out. Three kids were hanging out the windows and moving around inside the vehicle. (This was before car seat legislation.) The driver was not in the house long, and just like the caller said, she returned with a bag in her hands, and then backed out and drove away. This first event repeated itself time and time again. I jotted down each license number and a description of who went inside.

Just after five, I put down my notepad and pen. I recognized the woman who had just driven up. I watched as she went inside and watched as she came back out the door, with bag in hand, a few minutes later. "I'm going to find out what is going on, right now!" I said to myself as I started my unmarked police car and drove up behind the car in the driveway. The woman was my wife. Surprised to see me, she explained that she had recently gone to a Home Interiors party, one of those parties where people are shown products of one sort or another, and orders are taken for future delivery. The Home Interiors representative lived in the Santa Rita area home. The orders always came in on Thursday and people picked them up that afternoon.

* * *

"People of all ages are coming and going from a house down the street," said the second caller. "Cars started coming and going as soon as the two men moved in two weeks ago. It just doesn't look right. I know it isn't right."

"The caller knew it was a rent house, and she did know something wasn't right." I explained to my audience. "Because about noon, on a school day, the neighbor saw a girl streak out of the house and stop about halfway down the sidewalk. The teenager then danced around, laughed and held her arms up toward the sky, before she finally ran back into the house. The caller knew something was wrong, that the young person had to be high on something, because the young woman was naked from the waist up."

"Can you get license numbers for us, of the cars that come and go?" the caller was asked. "I'll do better than that," the caller said, "I've kept license numbers and descriptions ever since the guys moved there. I've got pages full."

After an intense investigation, probable cause was developed and the Narcs (detectives from the Narcotics Division) executed a search warrant on the house. The two men were arrested for selling methamphetamine, an illegal drug known as speed, crystal, meth, etc. One of the men was already on felony probation for doing the same thing.

You could have heard a pin drop after I told the last story. Nearly every person had been affected by drug abuse in one way or another, or knew someone who had. I finally closed with, "And don't assume that the police already know. Even though it may be common knowledge to you, the police may not know what you know. You may hold that one piece of evidence they need to put the bad guy in jail."

* * *

RUSSELL SMITH LOOKS OVER THE SCENE OF A HOUSE BURGLARY
THAT WAS PUBLICIZED AS A CRIME STOPPERS CRIME OF THE
WEEK. SAN ANGELO STANDARD-TIMES PHOTOGRAPH.

The Look

CRIME STOPPERS PUT MY FACE on television, my voice on the radio and my name regularly in the San Angelo Standard-Times. I couldn't go anywhere without someone stopping me and saying hello, or telling me something they thought we needed to know. When I was transferred into the narcotics division in 1983, I realized that being recognized could be a negative thing for a "Narc," and that I needed to change my appearance. I did several things to change that look.

My hair grew out pretty quickly and the beard followed suit. I hated the growth on the face because there was a period in which it itched like crazy. I let both grow out long and kept the color modified by meeting a beautician in a hair salon after the place closed. "What color do you want it now?" she would ask.

I realized that the "new look" worked when I went into a trailer house and bought a baggie of marijuana from a woman who would have otherwise known me. She started to get a little suspicious when I was headed out the door with the dope in my hand. "Put that down your pants, you don't want anyone to see it," she said, as I turned to look back at her. She must have caught something in my gaze, because she then said, almost under her breath, "Busted." She was right. She had almost a quarter pound of the stuff bagged and ready to sell inside her living room.

* * *

The look did have a negative impact on my relationships with good folks. It caused what today are two of my most precious memories.

I had become good friends with television personality Pat Attebery while I was the Crime Stoppers coordinator. We regularly saw each other at the KCTV television station and at various community events. Several months after I transferred into the narcotics division, I saw Pat talking to a group of people at Sunset Mall. I just had to say "hello."

I did just what I would have done when I was clean cut, wearing a suit and tie. I walked right up beside her but didn't interrupt. She kept on talking but immediately took a step away, realizing that some less desirable person had just violated her space. She didn't turn and look, though apparently keeping a close eye in her peripheral vision, she was visibly uncomfortable.

When I finally got a chance to speak, I said, "What's going on Pat?"

My friend recognized my voice. She turned and looked at me, and a big smile came across her face. I think she said, "Oh, you look terrible," and then we hugged, like we had so many times before.

* * *

My wife always sat in the choir loft, behind the pulpit, when we were at church on Sunday mornings. Our children sat with the other kids, in the middle near the front. The Church sanctuary actually had three sections of pews. Those on the left and right held about ten spaces, and the longer pews in the middle held more. I always sat on the left side, about half way down, with my shoulder against the outside framework of the pew. A group of ladies always sat to my right, on the other end, and a few sat behind and in front of them. It was a habit we had all developed over the years.

One Sunday, after I had grown the long hair and beard, I walked into the service a little late and positioned myself in the same seat I'd sat in for years. Then I realized that all the ladies were looking my way, and, apparently not recognizing me, they looked at each other, then stood and moved over to the pews within the middle of the sanctuary.

* * *

One not so precious moment occurred when I was in a trailer house in Grape Creek, discussing a dope deal with a pretty blonde who said her husband was bigger than a grizzly bear. I was trying to buy hashish, an illegal drug produced from the marijuana plant, but the girl said they were out at the time.

I smiled as the girl described how she hid the illegal drug beneath her buxomness as she periodically flew back to Texas from Kansas. I smiled because of her creativity and because I had a microphone hidden on my person. I knew my partner Steve Wilson was down the highway, listening, and recording the event. I knew the description of the criminal enterprise would make great evidence later.

I had not been there long when a man knocked on the door, and then came on inside. I don't know who was more surprised, he or I. I had arrested him during a drug raid the week before. I had actually put the cuffs on him. He knew I was a police officer, but he didn't say anything about it, probably because I'd put my hand behind my back, and felt the comfort of the revolver hidden there.

"Well, it's getting hot in here, (the signal to let my partner know something was not right), so I guess I'll get back with you later," I said as I stood to leave.

"You do that, I'll be making another run soon," said the tiny blonde, as she grabbed the ampleness where she said she hid the drugs.

I was never so glad to leave that trailer house that afternoon. Of course, no one had gotten hurt and I knew that my partner would have been there had things gone bad. At least that was what I thought until I saw him, with his hood up and DPS Trooper Tommy Matthews trying to jump his vehicle off, as I drove down the highway. His battery had shorted out when he plugged in the recording device. He'd never heard a word and nothing was recorded. We never were able to arrest the dope dealer.

* * *

DETECTIVE RUSSELL SMITH.
PHOTOGRAPH FROM FAMILY SCRAPBOOK.

The Phone Call

IT HAD ALREADY BEEN A hectic day. We, the narcotics detectives, executed a search warrant and found a quantity of heroin inside tiny balloons hidden inside a house. Two suspects were arrested and taken to jail. Steve Wilson had been the case agent, the officer who had obtained the search warrant. His phone rang later that afternoon. "Where? When? Okay, we'll be there," said Wilson.

Steve Wilson was a former DPS Trooper with previous experience arresting narcotics violators. Shortly after joining the police department, he was assigned to our narcotics section where we teamed up as partners. He was tall and thin and I was short and heavy-set.

"Let's go," Wilson said as he headed out the office door. And we were gone.

There is a saying that policemen are no better than who talks to them. This is especially true for detectives who investigated illegal drug activity. The phone call had been from one of Wilson's confidential informants, someone who had been reliable in giving him information about illegal narcotics in the past. He and I actually called such people spies. So we met Steve's spy and learned about a drug dealer who was in possession of a quantity of methamphetamine. For the sake of this story, we call the suspect Speedo.

The information was that Speedo was making deliveries of the illegal drug in the southwest part of the city. We knew the guy's name, description, color of his car and the license plate number. The other detectives were contacted and we all started to look for Speedo.

After we'd spent several hours looking for the guy, I was beginning to think our efforts might be for naught when my pager started buzzing. I hit the button and recognized the dispatch office phone number. We stopped at the convenience store at Sunset and Sul Ross so I could use the phone.

The pay phone was on the outside, attached to the northwest corner of the building. "A reporter called and wants to talk to you," said the dispatcher.

I dropped coins into the pay phone and dialed the number to the San Angelo Standard-Times. I vaguely remembered the woman's name. She was a newly hired reporter that I'd met the week before. She was now covering the police beat at night, while Bob Becknell, the regular police reporter, worked during the day.

"Can you give me the details of the drug bust?" the woman asked.

I started to explain that we were really busy and I didn't have time to discuss it now. I told her she would really need to talk to Steve because it was his search warrant, and then I heard a noise behind me. Steve was slapping the side of the car. His head was turned and he was looking directly across the street into the parking lot behind Southwest Plaza. I followed his gaze.

I could not believe my eyes. A car that looked just like the one we were looking for was driving across the parking lot right toward us. I started to explain to the reporter that I was going to have to talk to her later when I realized that Speedo was actually driving into the parking lot of the convenience store. The guy we were looking for actually drove up past our car and parked right beside the pay phone. When he opened the door and got out, he was just three feet away from me. He apparently planned to use the same pay phone that I was using.

I told the reporter that she'd have to hold on for just a minute and I dropped the phone. The next thing she heard was, "FREEZE! POLICE!"

Steve Wilson told the reporter that she'd have to call me later, that I was busy arresting somebody. She really didn't understand and thought that we were putting one over on her. On the other hand, Speedo, with methamphetamine in his shirt pocket, saw the badge and gun and realized the ordeal was real.

* * *

The Candy

STEVE WILSON WALKED INTO THE office carrying a foil covered paper plate. He lifted the edge and handed me a piece of his wife's scrumptious chocolate-covered-peanut candy. His wife really knew how to cook such things; you just wanted another, and another, and another. Yet I knew we'd have to wait because the first thing we did each morning was take the personal histories of any drug suspects who were arrested the night before.

A personal history involved asking a set of questions that basically gave us a glimpse into the person's life. The questions were pretty general: Name? Address? Date-of-birth? Where were you born? Who are your parents? How many brothers and sisters do you have? It was always interesting to know if they graduated from high school, or not. Over several years the majority of people arrested for drug violations had not gotten past the 10th grade. Finally we were finished, and I was ready to dig into the candy, however the phone rang and we had to leave.

The foil-covered plate was gone from Steve's desk when we returned several hours later. It was nowhere to be found and the candy was gone. Needless to say, I was disappointed and so were my taste buds.

It was several months before Steve walked into the office again with another foil covered paper plate. He lifted the edge and showed me what appeared to be the same chocolate-covered candy. When I reached for a piece, he pushed it away and whispered, "Whatever you do, don't eat any of this."

"Let's go script a house," he said aloud later, and he left the plate on his desk.

It was a common occurrence for detectives to go get a physical description of a drug dealer's house so it could be used on a search warrant affidavit. We drove by a particular house and used a tape recorder to define the color, numbers, direction the front door faced, and other identifiers that could lead anyone back to the location where drugs were possessed or sold. While we were gone, Steve didn't say a word about the candy.

The plate of candy was gone when we returned an hour later. There wasn't anyone else around either. Steve just smiled. I asked him what was in the candy, but he didn't answer. Whatever it was though, it cleaned out the place.

* * *

Police! Search Warrant!

I RAISED MY HAND AND swore to the accuracy of particular information before Justice of the Peace Ruth Nicholson. The typed pages I had given her described a suspected dope dealer, his place of residence and how I knew that he was selling heroin. After carefully reading the affidavit, she signed the search warrant.

"I have warrant in hand; let's meet at the station," I said over the encrypted radio frequency used by the narcotics detectives.

"Police! Search Warrant!" The three words that police officers love to say and drug dealers dread. Yet, unlike the movies or television shows, the means to obtain such a tool doesn't just come with the snap of your fingers. Specific requirements must be met before a Judge will ever authorize such a warrant.

The Fourth Amendment to the United States Constitution states, "... no Warrants shall issue, but upon probable cause, supported by Oath or affirmation, and particularly describing the place to be searched, and the person or things to be seized." Police officers who develop probable cause, the reasonable belief that a person has committed a crime, may produce a written document that describes the crime, person, place and probable cause, and the officer may swear to that affidavit before a Judge. A search warrant is the court order issued by a magistrate that authorizes law enforcement officers to conduct the search of a person or location for evidence of a criminal offense. It allows the seizure of unlawful items or evidence of a crime.

For safety reasons, we regularly met to discuss the way we would execute any search warrant. The "case agent," the officer who obtained the probable cause and knew about the suspected drug dealer, normally briefed the raid team about any weapons, innocent family members (especially children), and any information about the quantity of drugs and where they might be hidden. On this particular day, I said, "These addicts are especially paranoid, so we need to determine the best way to get to the house without being seen."

The white, wood-framed residence was just one house away from the corner. We decided to pack everyone inside one vehicle. The idea was to park on the opposite side of the neighbor's house, so we would not be seen until we were already in motion to enter the structure. The backyards were not fenced, so we would run behind the neighbor's house and around to the front of the suspect's house.

Once we got there, I would pull back the screen door, knock and yell "Police! Search Warrant!" If the nice dope dealer didn't open the door, Detective Jerry Cornelius would use one of his famous "mule kicks" so we could gain entry. Two team members would enter with us, while others would secure the back of the house and anyone outside. It was a simple plan. I knew it would work; I just knew it would.

We drove the van up to the opposite side of the neighbor's house. With a copy of the search warrant in my back pocket, I left the van first and ran around the back of the neighbor's house. As I rounded the front corner of the dope dealer's house, I could not believe my eyes. The screen door was the only door between the raid team and the inside of the residence. The front door was open. I threw the door aside, ran inside and yelled, "Police! Search Warrant!"

The dope dealer was in the living room, sitting before a small footstool, using a knife to slowly cut heroin away from its aluminum wrapper. He dropped the knife and raised his hands as I screamed, "Freeze!"

I realized we had him. We had the dope. I shouted, "Cuff him," as I kept my police revolver leveled on the guy.

Well, Mr. Dope Dealer must have thought I was crazy. He looked from side to side, and around me. Then I realized the raid team members were not there with me. I soon realized being short does have its advantages. Luckily no one was seriously hurt as I ran through the backyard; I hadn't even seen the clothesline.

* * *

Not For Everybody

THE ILLEGAL DRUG WORLD IS a dark place where money rules the day. It is a place where pretty only seems pretty, and lives are decimated almost as quickly as the tick of the clock. Officers who investigate such crimes take great risks, and the job is not for everybody. Though I took on the challenge, this assignment was really not a good thing for me.

I was the only one in the office when the phone rang. DPS Narcotics Agent Al Gonzales was on the other end, "A plane blipped the radar coming out of Mexico and it is going to land at Mathis Field. Can you meet me there?"

The small plane landed to refuel. Gonzales, DPS Intelligence Agent Enrique Garcia and I were there. Two men were detained and several packages were taken inside the nearby building. Agent Gonzales unwrapped several cigarette boxes and a paper sack; inside were tightly wrapped packs of one hundred dollar bills. It was the first time I'd actually seen $500,000 in cash. It made me realize that there are those who really do benefit from all the sadness of the illegal drug world.

* * *

"They're going to kill you," said an informant who had been credible in the past. I don't know how many times I heard those words, but this was one time that I took it to heart. The dope dealer was dangerous and capable.

"Pack for at least a week, maybe more," I told my wife who grew up in Rocksprings and was naïve about the life I had stepped into. My dear friends Ralph and Ethel "Mac" Ellis had agreed to allow my family to live with them, out toward Wall, until the threat passed. It was probably an adventure to the kiddos, but my wife began to realize the sacrifices caused by criminal investigations from the dark side. They lived with our friends for part of that year.

It was not long after my family moved back home that a woman called about three one morning. "Let me speak to Russell!" she demanded.

"He's not here," said my wife.

"Don't give me that. I saw him at Santa Fe Junction tonight. He was with some blonde. Now let me talk to him," said the woman who used about as many four letter words as not.

I was in Austin, and asleep at the time my wife got that call. I'd made the mistake of giving my home number to certain confidential informants. My wife was naturally upset and wished I were home, instead of waiting to testify before the Texas legislature.

Not everyone can maintain a healthy family life and work a heavy caseload as a narcotics detective. Linda had finally had enough by the end of 1984 and I moved into an apartment.

The challenge of arresting dope dealers has a thrill of its own. It grows on you. The criminals are trying to outsmart you, and you are doing what you can to build probable cause so you can arrest them. But in the end, it was my little boy's words that brought me back to reality – to what was really important in life. "Are you going to come visit us when we move?" I sent flowers and asked if I could come back home.

"When you answer that phone, you become another person. You talk a different language even though we are right here," said my wife when we sat down to talk about us getting back together. She laid down the rules that day. I was to get another phone and unplug the informant phone when I was not there. I was to take the sergeant's test and leave the narcotics assignment as soon as I was promoted.

I studied hard, scored high and was promoted in late 1985. Like I said, this assignment was not for everybody.

* * *

DPS Narcotics Agent Al Gonzales seized $500,000
in cash from a small plane at Mathis Field.
Shown is just one of many bundles of $100
bills. SAPD crime scene photograph.

The Honking Horn

"128, COMPLAINANT REPORTS A CAR horn keeping them awake in the area of Glenna and Nottingham. They (the complainant) don't want to talk."

It was nearly 3:00 a.m. I stopped in the parking lot of the convenience store at Arden and Glenna. I cut the engine and got out. After a few minutes, I heard a car horn blast several times not too far away. It stopped for just a second, and then did it again.

A yellow Cadillac was parked on Glenna just a block away from Arden Road. It was facing the large apartment complex with buildings on both sides of the street. As I drove toward it, with my window down, I could hear the noise again, and again.

I didn't recognize the car but did know the cowboy behind the wheel. "What's going on," I asked.

"Just waiting for my girlfriend," the man said as he tilted his head to the side so his straw hat would clear as he got out. I asked him to do several field sobriety tests because I could smell alcohol on his breath. He rolled up his long sleeves before he walked the straight line, stood on one leg and touched his nose.

"You passed the tests," I said, and he responded with, "I'm just honking the horn to let my new girlfriend know that I'm outside."

"But why don't you just go to the door to get her?" I asked.

He smiled, nodded toward a pretty little blonde who was running toward us and sarcastically said, "I don't think her husband would like it very much."

* * *

SGT. RUSSELL SMITH HELPS INVENTORY A CAR AFTER A
PATROL OFFICER MAKES AN ARREST. SAPD PHOTO.

Mr. Williams

ONLY THREE HOURS INTO THE shift, about 11:00 p.m., the dispatcher assigned Officer J.D. Carter to help with a patient problem at a local nursing home.

"10-4," Carter answered. The tires squealed against the asphalt as he turned his police car around and headed toward his assigned location. Less than a minute later, the dispatcher updated the call, "the patient left the nursing home and is walking south." He put his headlights on bright and activated his overhead lights.

The year was 1987 and Carter was in his third year with the San Angelo Police Department. The busy night shift had allowed him to see almost everything. The good-natured protector saw the man's white shirt while he was still a block away. He also saw the scurrying motions of the three uniformed nurses. He pulled over onto the shoulder, on the opposite side of the roadway and stopped in front of the man and his pursuers.

The man's wrinkled face and eyebrows squinted against the flashing lights. He dropped his head slightly as Carter approached. His white shirt was actually a tucked-in hospital gown, followed by khaki pants and slip-on house shoes. A somewhat torn and bent dirty straw hat sat atop his head. Dark blotches were visible on the back of the man's hands, as were calluses from years of hard work. The tips of his fingers were yellow-brown from years of smoking roll-your-own cigarettes. His build was thin, yet what some might describe as wiry. Carter, at six feet, stood eye to eye with the man.

The man was quiet as the three nurses chorused almost in unison, "Now you make Mr. Williams come back with us. He's being a bad boy, you make him come home."

The man sighed somewhat, removed his hat and held it to his chest, beneath crossed arms. He leaned against the front fender of the police car and just shook his head.

The women were still chattering as I parked across the street. Carter raised his eyes toward the sky to signal that this was one of "those." He'd heard the women's story. The man had lived in the nursing home for several years. It was after bedtime and no one was allowed to go out. They locked the doors at 10:30, but the doors had push bars in case of fire. There were no commitment papers, but the rules didn't allow anyone to go out after the scheduled bedtime.

J.D. took charge and said in a firm tone, "You ladies go over there and talk to the Sarge while I talk to Mr. Williams." The women seemed kind of put-off by the command, but did as they were told.

Mr. Williams, it turned out, was seventy-nine years old. He owned a ranch in his younger days, but lost it during the 50's drought. His wife died about 1981. He had three kids, two sons and a daughter, but they lived in other states. As Mr. Williams put it, "They got their own lives to live." His oldest son, who was a law-yer, had helped him move into the nursing home, two years and five months before. Mr. Williams thought it would be best because the kids wouldn't have to worry about him.

J.D. noticed the man's mind was still very much intact, so much in fact that the investigation became a conversation. Mr. Williams explained that he was not running away and apologized for, as he put it, "Causing such a ruckus, to waste you boys' time. I was jus' headed to the store to get some makings, they haven't let me have a smoke in a long time."

Mr. Williams hung his head and said, as if to himself rather than to the policeman, "I'd even thought about going up to that restaurant on Bryant Boulevard and getting me a real hamburger. I'm kinda' tired of the same ol' food, week after week."

I'd listened to the nurses concerns, but told them to wait while I talked to Officer Carter. As I approached, he looked at me with questioning eyes. I knew J.D. was a caring man who had an idea how he wanted to rectify the situation. We talked for a few minutes, then I turned toward Mr. Williams and, in a somewhat strong voice, said, "Mr. Williams, Officer Carter will give you a ride back, while I escort the nurses."

The old man put his straw hat back on, straightened it some, and moved toward the passenger side of the police car. J.D. Carter helped him into the front seat.

I loaded the three nurses into my patrol car and headed toward the nursing home. I watched in my rear view mirror as Carter turned his patrol car around and headed in the opposite direction. I explained that patrol officers were required to write reports and that Mr. Williams would be along shortly, after all the information was collected and written down.

As I dropped off the caregivers, I hoped the convenience store still sold Bugler and wondered if the old man would have French fries with his hamburger.

* * *

The Epilogue

ONE POLICEMAN'S LIGHTS AND SIREN is a collection of memories from my early police career. These were the first stories that came to mind when I started to jot a few things down. Of course, there are many more, a few that I'll mention before I close.

Police officers learn many things about people's lives. Sometimes that knowledge comes during the worst of times in a citizen's life, or just by happenstance. The latter brings to mind something that happened while I was a lake ranger.

It was a beautiful morning in early 1979. I was patrolling the pasture area around the south pool of Twin Buttes Reservoir. I noticed an El Camino off the beaten path; an El Camino that I realized belonged to someone I knew, someone I knew was married. Another vehicle was nearby. I started to drive toward them, until I saw legs and realized I would interfere in an intimate moment. I thought about the guy's wife and kids. I turned around and drove away.

About an hour later, parked on a dirt road that led from the lake to the highway, I saw the same two vehicles headed toward me. I didn't look directly at the El Camino at first, didn't want the guy to know that

I had seen what I had seen, but finally did look as I raised a hand to wave. Nobody was more surprised than I. It was the guy's wife. I didn't know the younger man in the other car.

* * *

During our patrol briefing one Christmas Eve, not too long after I was promoted to Sergeant, I told the officers what so many supervisors before me had said, "Don't arrest anybody, unless you just have to, because it's Christmas." The weather caused me to say something else, "Everything is supposed to ice over around midnight, so get on a parking lot and don't wreck any cars."

When it was already an hour into Christmas and sleet was falling, I noticed a car with only one working headlight coming down the street. Parked beside a convenience store, I didn't give the weather any thought as I put my patrol unit in gear and pulled onto the roadway. The one-eyed car drove north, and then turned east.

The vehicle stopped in front of a house just a block off the main thoroughfare. Two little kids jumped out and ran for the front door. I pulled up behind, turned on my overhead emergency lights and put the car in park. The driver rolled down her driver's side window.

"Ma'am, you have a headlight out, you ought to get it checked," I said to the young mother behind the steering wheel. I already had my weight shifted to my right foot, ready to walk back to my car and drive away.

The scream that came out of the woman's mouth was deep and guttural. Her head and shoulder length hair started shaking from side to side. Her hands started pounding the steering wheel so hard that it didn't sound like flesh against plastic. Then she slammed her fists straight up into the headliner, over and over again. And the groans of agony, the sounds of total abandon brought her daddy out of the house.

I put my hands up and started backing away, out into the middle of the street. The man, wearing only a tee shirt and jeans, was looking right at me; coming with a purpose like a lioness would to protect her cubs. He was at the curb when everything became quiet.

"Go back in the house Daddy! I NEED to talk to the policeman!" said the woman in a firm voice.

Her daddy looked at her, as if questioning what was going on, but she used her hand to whisk him back.

It was really cold and the sleet was getting heavier. The roads were slick. The woman said she needed to talk to someone, to me, and I suggested we do so in my patrol car where it was warm.

The woman had been at a wonderful time in her life. Married to a man who had a good job, with two wonderful kids and a great house, she had taken the children to spend Christmas with her husband's parents because he had to work. They had opened presents early on Christmas Eve before the wife and kiddos headed back home to surprise the husband and daddy.

The woman parked in the back of the house and went in to get help with the sleeping siblings. Only instead of her surprising the husband, she got the surprise. She found him with another woman, a woman she knew.

The look in her eyes and on her face that morning revealed the greatest low she'd ever known. She was hurt beyond any understanding. She seemed to go into shock,

at times, and life didn't seem to mean much in those mo-
ments. We talked for nearly two hours; it was after three
when she finally got out and went into the house.

I've always wondered if God put my car in gear that
night. I saw the woman several years later and she
seemed to be doing okay. Her kids had grown, were
taller. She was surviving. I think of her every time I see
a vehicle with only one headlight, and every time I wish
her the best.

* * *

Men and women in the police profession see the worst
in society and rarely the best. Each officer has their own
stories that are exciting, sad, unique or funny, though
the majority would deal with a part of society that most
everyone else will never see, or would rather forget. I
realized this early on...

Untitled

Shots and screams,
Hurt and death, and
Pain and cruelty.

You might peek outside,
As you make sure your doors and windows are secure;
But the peace officer will end up
Without any doors between him and the problem.

Russell S. Smith
Copyright 1984

"125, 131, 126, shooting, two down, ambulance on the way," reported the dispatcher.

The small bar was just north of downtown. Normally a quiet watering hole, the place was especially busy when I followed Officer Jimmie Byrne through the front door.

The jukebox was playing; people were dancing and playing pool. The bartender gave several longneck beers to the waitress. She stepped across two bodies on the floor as she made her way across the room to deliver them. People were talking, laughing, socializing and yet two men had just been shot and blood was starting to pool on the concrete. "I believe it was Sgt. Kirby Poss who pulled the plug on the music," said Jimmie Byrne.

Emergency medical technicians (San Angelo firemen) followed us inside and started to care for the victims. We started to interview the witnesses; I started at the back of the room.

"I was in the bathroom," said the first person I questioned. So did everyone else as I went around the room. Finally, I knelt down and talked to a little boy who was watching his dad play pool. "Did you see what happened?" I asked.

"The man came in and shot those men," the child answered.

"Do you know who the man was?" I continued.

"Daddy said it was…" said the boy who identified the suspect.

The child told us the shooter left, walking north. The information was relayed to officers investigating outside. Detectives eventually took over the investigation.

All these years later, I don't know for sure what happened to the victims or if the suspect was ever arrested. But I do know that many times over the years we talked about the waitress stepping over the bodies and about everyone being in the bathroom. In the police psyche, we would always laugh – because each of us knew the bathroom only accommodated one person.

Untitled

Sometimes I joke about things
That are not funny at all:
And you say, "Boy your job sure
Has deranged your mind;"
But what you don't realize is
That if I didn't laugh and joke,
Then I would most assuredly cry.

Russell S. Smith
Copyright 1984

In the fall of 2009, I learned that my career with the San Angelo Police Department almost didn't happen. Retired Lt. Tom Flowers told me that two people on the oral review board didn't want to hire me. "They thought you were too little. We discussed it at length before you were ever interviewed."

Luckily, I was hired, and I've never forgotten something Tom Flowers told me just before he retired, "I wish I could have spent my last year on patrol, so I would never forget why I did this in the first place."

* * *

RUSSELL POSES WITH HIS KIDS, SHANNON AND RYAN,
EARLY IN HIS POLICE CAREER. FAMILY PHOTO.

The Policeman's Prison

Sometimes
    I have let
    A few close enough
    To feel
    My body heat.
Sometimes
    I feel their warmth
    See their understanding
    Want the existence
    Need the occasion.
But no fear
    It is still there,
    The ever present
    Unbiased protecting
    Cold wall
    Between myself
    And those outside,
And as time passes
    The wall grows stronger
    The coldness within facades
    And becomes natural.
Sometimes
    I would like to let
    Someone near.

Russell S. Smith
©1984

About The Author

Russell S. Smith was born in Uvalde, Texas to parents Dick and June Smith. He started writing poems and short stories long before he graduated from Uvalde High School in 1969. He attended Southwest Texas Junior College, Howard College and Angelo State University; the majority of his classes dealt with criminal justice.

His law enforcement career began as a reserve deputy with the Tom Green County Sheriff's Department and ended when he retired as the San Angelo Texas Police Chief in 1999. This experience spurred his professional writing career when he sold his first article to a police trade magazine in 1980.

Russell spent five years as an outdoor columnist for the San Angelo Standard-Times and several magazines. He received numerous awards for his writing and photography from the Texas Outdoor Writers' Association. His first nonfiction book, **The Gun That Wasn't There**, was published in 2007. His second, **No Reason to Kill**, the search for Sheila Elrod's killer, was published in 2008. **One Policeman's Lights and Siren** is his third.

He continues to research and write nonfiction books from his home in San Angelo where he and his wife reside. (www.russellssmith.com)

Endnotes

[i] Russell S. Smith, service history, Texas Commission on Law Enforcement Officer Standards and Education, print date March 19, 2009.

[ii] Alan Sayre, staff writer, San Angelo Standard, Thursday, October 5, 1978.

[iii] Booking Records, Tom Green County Sheriff's Department.

[iv] San Angelo Standard-Times, August 7, 1978.

[v] Alan Sayre, staff writer, San Angelo Standard, October 5, 1978.

[vi] Russell S. Smith, Basic Law Enforcement Officers certificate, Texas Engineering Extensive Service, The Texas A&M University System, October 6, 1978.

[vii] San Angelo Standard-Times, October 7, 1978.

[viii] San Angelo Standard-Times, October 2, 1978.

[ix] Russell S. Smith, service history record, Texas Commission on Law Enforcement Officer Standards and Education, March 19, 2009.

Made in the USA
Charleston, SC
26 February 2010